War Record

of the

University Press, Oxford

THE UNIVERSITY PRESS, OXFORD

War Record

of the

University Press

Oxford

Oxford

Printed at the University Press

1923

FOREWORD

From the firing of the first gun in the great fight for freedom and the safety of the community, to the signing of the Armistice, the men of the Oxford University Press answered ungrudgingly to the nation's call, whether for service abroad, for army service at home, or for special work at Walton Street. A number of trained men, moved by patriotism and lofty ideals, went into the ranks immediately on the declaration of war, and were followed by other men from time to time, as calls were made, until 356 had gone. At the same time many who were too old or were otherwise unfit for active service were requisitioned for war printing, the resources of the Press being at times taxed to the utmost to print the reports and documents which played no mean part in securing the final victory.

The names of the forty-five whose lives were given to the cause are recorded on the Memorial erected in the Quadrangle by their fellow-workers. It is beyond our power adequately to honour them; they have honoured us for ever by the sacrifice they made. We recognize the debt we owe to them; and we do not forget the debt we owe to those who faced the same deadly perils and survived, most of them to return to us. Let us now consign to oblivion all hatred and bitterness, and devote ourselves to the nobler task of restoring goodwill and fellowship with all men.

The compilation of this record of the War services of the Walton Street Staff of the Oxford University Press has been a labour of love on the part of the indefatigable editor of *The Clarendonian*, Mr. A. Hinson, and others. That it makes its appearance so long after the Armistice is due to circumstances beyond their control.

F. J. H.

April 1923.

NOTE

The Roll of Service contained herein includes the name of every man who joined up from the Press: in other respects it is of necessity imperfect and incomplete; the desire to give in every instance an adequate record is not fulfilled. In so far as success has been attained it is due in very large measure to the generous help received from Mr. E. L. Gass, Mr. A. J. Bowen, Mr. C. E. Bowen, Mr. W. Collier, Mr. F. J. Ayres, and many others, as well as to the courtesy of the men themselves or of their relatives. My own part has been the endeavour of one, debarred from every recognized form of service, to pay worthy tribute to the many who served so well.

ALLPRESS HINSON.

CONTENTS

ILLUSTRATIONS

ON ACTIVE SERVICE

Being a brief record of the contribution of the Oxford members of the Oxford University Press in the Great War

THE Press at Oxford had just closed down for the annual holiday, when the crash came and Europe passed from peace to war. The local Territorials who 'proceeded' to Marlow on Sunday, 2 August 1914, for the annual fortnight's camp, were back at head-quarters on the following morning. A few hours later, on 4 August, the state of war was in being and nearly sixty mobilized Press men were 'on active service'.

The abrupt transition from the peaceful pursuit of trade necessarily obscured the outlook in all directions and substituted perplexity for plain sailing. For the management of the Press, as for other captains of industry, it raised problems entirely new and urgently pressing, and it may be that only those of the inner circle—those that remain—are fully aware of the resolute will that faced those problems and solved them. The Press organization was adapted to the unprecedented conditions with surprising promptness, and it was made possible to keep the large but dwindling staff employed. To say that the almost inevitable 'short time' was limited to about three weeks in the second month of the War is to do no more than hint at the tribute due to the management. New orders were found, or created, to fill the place of orders suspended, and the ordinary course of work gave place in an increasing degree to publications that contributed to the common cause, the winning of the War. In *The Clarendonian* issued a few weeks after the end of the War it was remarked: 'The Press has come through the severe ordeal of war-time astonishingly well. The pilots of the business have steered it through treacherous shoals, always with an eye to the safety of the crew; and . . . it will not be denied that, throughout the increasing strain, to many a worker the lines have fallen in less pleasant places than the Oxford University Press.'

Nor were the rank and file slow to adapt themselves to the altered situation. Their problems were different but not less difficult, and 'the men were splendid'. Their response to the country's call was spirited. The number on active service quickly passed the 100, reached 150 by Christmas, 200 before the end of 1915, 300 in the summer of 1917, and at the date of the Armistice stood at 356. With regard to enlistments in the later years it will not be forgotten that these were either youths who waited only until they attained military age, or men due for service because of the extension of the age-limit.

Of the 356 men, two were reservists, C. Davis and J. A. Timms; the latter went to France in the first Expeditionary Force, and holds the Mons Star. Two others (at least) were in France before the end of 1914. The first big draft of Press men to be sent abroad went out in the 1/4th Bn. of the Oxford & Bucks L.I. Mr. R. W. Chapman, at that time Assistant Secretary to the Delegates of the Press and an 'indispensable' in the piloting of the business on to the new lines, took up a commission as soon as the new order was established, and served as a gunner for over three years with the Salonika Force. A. Harris also was an officer from the commencement of his service. Seven others attained officers' rank, and it is worth noting that six of these seven had enlisted whilst yet in their apprenticeship; one of the six (Brocks) died, a prisoner of war in Asia Minor. The Roll includes one Guardsman (Edgington, killed in action), twelve who served in the Navy (two of these having first seen service in the Army), and one, a Belgian, who served in the forces of his native land. These men went to practically every front: it is not too much to claim that wherever the British Army was represented the Press was represented too.

Instances of relatives within the 356 include one, probably rare, of three generations on service at the same time. Recruiting Colour-Sergeant J. L. Surman was a familiar figure in the City from the beginning of the War, and the number of recruits enrolled by him was well over two thousand. His nephew, two sons, and a grandson, are included in this Roll. Of the six Fosters, four are brothers, and the other two

(C. and J.) are brothers and are cousins of the four. The four Goddards are brothers. There are three brothers Bowen (A. J., C. E., W. J.); three brothers Cleaver, as well as a cousin (R. A.); three brothers Kislingbury; and three brothers Lapworth. The latter trio were included in the mobilization on the outbreak of war. Instances of two brothers are numerous: they include F. W. and H. S. Chapman, sons of Mr. Frank Chapman, both of whom were killed.

In addition to the soldiers and sailors, two of the Oxford staff were engaged on National Service. Mr. T. Bruce, M.A., served in the War Trade Intelligence Department from March 1917 to June 1917, and in the Intelligence Department of the Admiralty from June 1917 to December 1919. Percy J. Green was employed on secret submarine construction at Southampton from September 1915 to Armistice Day.

The death-roll at the date of the Armistice was forty-four; one (R. G. Jones) succumbed later, and his name is inscribed with the others on the War Memorial.

Of the War's indirect toll among the personnel of the Press at home no exact record is possible; but who can doubt that the stress of the dark years was a contributory cause of the deaths of some who have passed away since 1914?—of the late Controller, Mr. Horace Hart, whose advancing years placed him among the earliest to yield under the tension; of the manager, Mr. George Denton, whose broad shoulders carried a big burden of responsibility and whose selfless devotion to the interests of the Press and to the national cause overtaxed even his sturdy powers; of Mr. Charles Cannan, the late Secretary to the Delegates, who lived to pilot the business through the years of war and to welcome home the returning soldiers and point out the way to avoid the rocks ahead. Remembered too are the veteran Mr. J. C. Pembrey, oriental reader, for over seventy years at the Press; Mr. Philip Molyneux, the editor of the *University Gazette*; Mr. W. S. Gibson, who succeeded Mr. W. R. F. Shilleto as a classical reader; Mr. W. A. Goodger, overseer of the Bookbinding and Warehouse Departments; 'Dick' Aldridge, overseer of the Stereotype Department; 'Jack' Webb, of the Counting House staff; 'Jack' Masters, pressman; 'Teddy' Taylor, clicker; 'Jack' Tyrrell, and others.

THE MEMORIAL SERVICE

This devotional Service to commemorate the fallen was held on the north side of the Quadrangle in the afternoon of 21 July 1919, and was conducted by the Very Rev. the Dean of Christ Church (Dr. T. B. Strong, now Bishop of Ripon). The impressiveness of the brief ceremony was intensified by the size of the gathering, which numbered nearly a thousand and included many relatives and friends of the men commemorated; by the sympathetic and helpful words of the Dean; and, not least, by the excellence of the music. The singing was led by a choir of Press vocalists, with choir boys from the churches of St. Giles and St. Michael, and the Press Orchestra at its best. The opening hymn, 'O God, our help in ages past', was followed by special prayers, the Twenty-third Psalm, and a Lesson, and the Dean then read the names of the forty-four men, as follows:

Let us remember with thanksgiving, and with all honour before God and men, the Officer, Non-commissioned Officers, and Men of the University Press who have died, giving their lives in the service of their country:

Charles Barfoot
John Best
James Blake
Archibald Bowen
Archibald Brocks
Arthur Burden
Frank Chapman
Horace Chapman
William Clack
William Cooper
William Draper
Percy Edgington
Frederick Fisher
George Fuller
Claude George
Geoffrey Green
Frederick Gulliver
Arthur Hiles
Harry Hill
William Howkins
Ernest Jago
David Jones
Percy Kench
Frederick Kerry
Richard Kimber
Aubrey Kitchen
Charles Kitchen
Percival Lines

Albert Margetts	Albert Simmonds
Herbert Miller	Joseph Simms
Ernest Panting	Thomas Surman
Henry Partridge	Henry Wakelin
Owen Price	William Wallen
Albert Rawlings	Bernard White
Ernest Schofield	Alfred Winstone
Richard Shrimpton	Douglas Woodward

Further prayers followed, and the hymn, 'Let saints on earth in concert sing'; and the Dean then delivered a very telling address from Rev. ii. 17: 'To him that overcometh, to him will I give of the hidden manna, and I will give him a white stone, and upon the stone a new name written, which no man knoweth but he that receiveth it.' The Service concluded with the hymn, 'For all the saints who from their labours rest', the Benediction, and the 'Last Post' and 'Réveillé'.

THE WAR MEMORIAL

The proposal to erect a permanent Memorial in the Quadrangle 'To the memory of the men of the Oxford University Press who died for their country in the Great War' was taken up with vigour. A committee was appointed, and the unspent balance of £23 from the Christmas Comforts Fund became the nucleus of the War Memorial Fund. Collections made in the various departments realized over £58, and a further £57 came in from the Second Food-Production Show. Donations &c. raised the total to £152, and the required sum of £176 was completed by a share of the proceeds of the Third Show.

In September 1920, at a meeting held at the Institute, preparations were initiated for the Unveiling Ceremony, and the Controller (presiding) foreshadowed the publication of this War Record.

The Unveiling of the Memorial took place on Tuesday, 5 October 1920, and again the very large gathering included many relatives and friends of the men commemorated. It may be recalled that amongst others who attended was Sir Walter Raleigh, then engaged on his *History of the War in the Air*, a work to which his life was sacrificed. After the opening hymn, 'O God, our help in ages past', the Controller, speaking for the War Memorial Committee, recalled the impressive Service held in that Quadrangle in July 1919. That expression of regret for the loss of brave comrades (he said) was now to be carried a step further. The names of those comrades had been graven in stone and placed close by the workrooms—a perpetual reminder that the liberties we still enjoyed were due in no small measure to the great price those men had paid. We should miss them in the workrooms, and we should always have a deep sympathy with the family circles where the gaps would be painfully felt. The Memorial was now to be unveiled, and it was fitting that that ceremony should be performed by one who was closely connected with the War work of the Press, as well as with the prosecution of the War.

Admiral Sir Reginald Hall then addressed the gathering as follows:

While it is always a distinction to be invited to take part in any function connected with your city, I regard it as an unusual honour that you should have asked me to participate in this afternoon's poignant but memorable ceremony. One fear, however, I have, that I doubt my ability to pay adequate tribute to the heroes, and fear that the reputation of those brave men might be imperilled either by my ignorance or by the exaggeration of my speech.

As to the former, those among us who were familiar with the men commemorated by this memorial will silently supply my deficiency; as to the latter, it seems impossible for any speaker, however gifted, to pay too lofty a tribute to the men who gave their lives in a war which has never been equalled for its demands upon human fortitude and courage.

Seven years ago none of the men associated with the Clarendon Press had any prevision of to-day's ceremony. They little thought that this afternoon we should be assembled in this familiar quadrangle to unveil a memorial inscribed with their names. Yet it is not surprising that we are so engaged. When the call to arms resounded through the nation, nowhere was the response more immediate or unreserved than in our universities. How speedily Oxford's four thousand undergraduates dwindled to two or three hundred, and the ancient peace of the college quadrangles was broken by the sharp commands of drill sergeants and the tramp of men in khaki!

THE WAR MEMORIAL

It was wholly natural for the men of this Press to respond with equal alacrity to their country's call. You are as pledged as they to those high ideals. You are in daily contact with the great literature not merely of distant ages and lands but also with that of your own country. In the 'Bible Side' you are familiar with the divine philosophy of life; in the 'Learned Side' you are in constant communion with the human wisdom of the ages. We are here this afternoon to pay our tribute to the memory of those who died that 'the flood of British freedom should not perish in bogs and sands'. Have they not richly earned the eulogy of Pericles: 'They gave their lives for the common weal, and in so doing won for themselves the praise which grows not old and the most distinguished of all sepulchres—not that in which they lie buried, but that in which their glory survives in everlasting remembrance.'

While, however, we recall with affectionate gratitude the war-services of those men of the Press who made the supreme sacrifice, I seize on this opportunity to express the nation's indebtedness to those other services of the Press which though less hazardous were of vital importance in winning the War. Some of those services were of a nature which depended on the skill, rapidity, and secrecy of execution. In none of those did this great Press fail. The printed page never played so important a part in war, and that weapon you supplied in abundance.

Such ceremonies as these are, one is glad to know, frequently being held in different parts of the country. Nothing is more natural than that each community, whether it be the village unit of our national life or the great city, shall honour their gallant dead. But I am sure you will agree with me when I say that these ceremonies will fail of part of their purpose unless they enable us to recapture something of that spirit of devotion, of that community of interest and lofty self-sacrifice which inspired us during the War.

During the War, and particularly in those dark days when the victory of the Allied cause seemed far off, it really appeared as though two thousand years of the teaching of the gospel of love was at last to bear its richest fruit; the capacity for brotherhood appeared to be realized by all; in the face of a common peril and amid the glowing light of sacrifice, we were so united in spirit and effort that we stood on the threshold of a new social order. Unhappily that light has since faded. The gospel of love has given place to a melancholy revival of class division and class hatred. Such memorials as this are a stern rebuke to any faithlessness to our ideals.

What we require to-day, if we are to honour our dead with more than stone memorials and lip-service, is that we strive to the utmost to awaken in peace time that heightened spirit which was evoked during the stress of the War. Perhaps we are too much inclined to place unreasoning faith in the mere machinery of reconstruction. We may, for example, be counting too much upon the far-off results of legislative measures, but 'if the world needs changing, we cannot leave the task simply to a better educated posterity. We must expect more from ourselves'.

To order our lives in the spirit of the men whom we commemorate to-day will be the highest tribute we can pay to their memory. You have wisely chosen for the form of this memorial that altar-shaped model which is so eloquent of the purpose to which it is devoted. But there is sacrifice in life as well as in death. Let us resolve as we pass this stone from day to day to make of our daily task an offering in the service of the community and nation which have been preserved to us by the life-blood of our own comrades.

Sir Reginald then unveiled the Memorial, and the Rev. W. E. Sherwood offered the dedicatory prayers.

Dr. Hogarth (for the Delegates of the Press) said it was Sir Reginald Hall who gave the Press its great opportunities of industrial service in war time. The work was done under strange conditions, but it could not have been done with a higher standard of efficiency and honour by any body of men. The Delegates wished to be associated with the tribute to the fallen and with the sympathy called forth by their loss.

The Service concluded with the singing of 'Fight the good fight' and the sounding of the 'Last Post'.

ROLL OF SERVICE[1]

Alder, J. (Machine Room, wash-house). Enlisted on 8 Nov. 1917. Served in England in the 92nd Res. Bn. Hants Regt. to Mar. 1918, and in France in the 22nd London Regt. from Apr. 1918 to Apr. 1919, and then in the 13th Middlesex Regt. to 14 Oct. 1919. At Albert, 1 May; Combles, 1–2 Sept.; Montaucourt, 17 Oct.; Lille, 6 Nov. 1918.

Allsworth, T. (Machine Room, feeder, Miehle). Enlisted on 2 Mar. 1915. Served in England in the 2/4th Oxf. & Bucks L.I. until 24 June 1916, and thenceforward in France in the 10th Lincs Regt. In engagements on the Somme in Aug., and Armentières in Nov. 1916; Arras (May), St. Quentin (Aug.), Passchendaele (Oct.), 1917; Croiselles, Mar. 1918. Wounded and taken prisoner in the latter engagement, remaining in the enemy's hands (at Münster, Rennbahn, Westphalia) to 6 Dec. Subsequently served in England in the 4th Lincs Regt. until discharge. Wounded in hip (at St. Quentin) and in ear and eye (Croiselles). Discharged, blind right eye, 26 Mar. 1919. Resumed work at the Press.

Andrews, D. G. (Warehouse). Enlisted on 6 Nov. 1916. Served in England in the 4th Roy. Berks Regt. and in the 10th Oxf. & Bucks L.I. to July 1917; in the Roy. Wilts Yeomanry (on the East Coast) to end of year; and (in Ireland) in the 1st Res. Garr. Bn. Worc. Regt. from 11 Jan. 1918 to demobilization. Appointed Lance-Corpl. Demobilized on 23 Jan. 1919. Resumed work at the Press.

Ayres, F. J. D. (Monotype Staff, keyboard). [Previous Service in the 2nd V.B. Oxf. L.I. from Apr. 1903 to Apr. 1908, and thenceforward in the 4th Oxf. & Bucks L.I., T.F.] Mobilized with the 4th Oxf. & Bucks L.I. (M.G. Sergt.) on 4 Aug. 1914, and served in England in that unit until 28 Mar. 1915. Went to France with the 48th (South Midland) Divisional Transport on 28 Mar. 1915. Transferred to the M.G. Corps 11 Jan. 1916; returned to England 8 Aug. 1917, and served on the M.G. Corps Instructional Staff from that date onward. Engagements included the Second Battle of Ypres, 1915; the Somme, Aug.–Dec. 1916; the advance

[1] Medals awarded for specially meritorious service or conspicuous gallantry are mentioned in these records so far as they are known; but the 1914–15 Star, Victory Medal, General Service Medal, and Territorial War Medal may in general be inferred from the details given and are omitted here.

(Peronne), Mar. 1917; St. Julien and Steenbeck, July 1917. Promoted C.S.M. 1 Nov. 1916; appointed C.S.M.I., M.G. School, Officers' Wing, Oct. 1918; A./R.S.M., N.C.O.'s School, M.G.T.C., Belton Park, Aug. 1918. Awarded the Meritorious Service Medal, Jan. 1917. Demobilized on 11 Jan. 1919, and resumed work at the Press. [Still serving in the 4th Oxf. & Bucks L.I. as C.S.M.]

Ayres, G. W. (Monotype Staff, keyboard). Enlisted in the Oxf. & Bucks L.I. on 21 Oct. 1916, serving in England until 5 Jan. 1917. Sailed for India on 6 Jan., and proceeded thence to Mesopotamia with the 1st Oxf. & Bucks L.I. (43rd) on 25 May, remaining in that country for a year and a half. Subsequently in Macedonia from 10 Dec. 1918 to Oct. 1919. Demobilized on 17 Oct. 1919. Resumed work at the Press.

Baldwin, A. E. (Machine Room, wash-house). Enlisted in the Oxf. & Bucks L.I. on 8 Nov. 1915. Served in England, with intervals of ill health, to June 1916, when he was discharged. Subsequently served intermittently to 12 Dec. 1917. In France in the London Rifle Brigade from 28 Sept. 1918 to the following July. Demobilized 25 July 1919.

Bampton, C. (Machine Room, feeder, Miehle). Enlisted on 17 Jan. 1917. Served in the R.E. in England (Sig.) to 17 June, and in France from 21 June to 28 Aug. 1917. Gassed. In hospital and convalescent, and on Home Service from 18 Feb. to 25 Nov. 1918. To Russia, in the 27th Div. Sig. Coy., 25 Nov. 1918. Promoted Corpl., July 1919. Demobilized on returning to England.

† Barfoot, C. M. (Monotype Staff, compositor). Enlisted in the Oxf. & Bucks L.I. on 1 Sept. 1914 and posted to the 7th Bn. Served in England to 15 Oct. 1915; in France from 16 Oct. to Dec.; and in Salonika from Dec. 1915 until his death. Appointed Lance-Corpl.; promoted Corpl. Killed in action in Salonika on 25 Apr. 1917.

Barson, H. (Machine Room, Miehle). Enlisted in Oct. 1915 in the A.S.C., serving in England for about three weeks, and then in Salonika until March 1919. Demobilized on return to England. Resumed work at the Press.

Bayliss, F. (Type Foundry). Enlisted in the Oxf. & Bucks L.I. on 20 July 1916, serving in England in the 3rd Bn. to the November following. Posted to the 2nd Bn. (52nd) in France on 9 Nov. 1916, and was in several engagements (Somme, Arras, and others). Injured in attack at Oppy Wood on 28 Apr. 1917 (buried by explosion: crushed back, concussion). Under medical treatment in England for six months. Transferred on 24 Oct. 1917 to the R.F.A., serving in Ireland until demobilized on 20 Mar. 1919. Resumed work at the Press.

Beal, G. (Stereo and Electro Room, finisher). [Previous Service in Territorials for three years.] Mobilized with the 4th Oxf. & Bucks L.I. on 4 Aug. 1914. Proceeded to France with the 1/4th Bn. on 29 Mar. 1915. Served in France, M.G. Section, until discharged, time-expired, on 20 May 1916. Resumed work at the Press.

Beal, W. (B.S. Composing Room, apprentice). [Previous Service in the 4th Oxf. & Bucks L.I. from Nov. 1912.] Mobilized with the 4th Oxf. & Bucks L.I. on 4 Aug. 1914. Served in England in the 1/4th Bn. to Oct. 1914, and in the 2/4th Bn. thenceforward. In France (with 2/4th Bn.) from 24 May 1916 to 4 Apr. 1919. Engagements: Fromelles, 19 July 1916; Somme, Nov. 1916; Passchendaele Ridge, Aug. 1917; Cambrai, Dec. 1917; St. Quentin, 21 Mar. 1918; Cambrai, Oct. 1918. Appointed Lance-Corpl., May 1916; promoted Corpl., Aug. 1918. Demobilized on 5 May 1919. Resumed work at the Press.

Beesley, A. J. (B.S. Office). Enlisted on 16 Oct. 1916. Posted to the Roy. Warwick Regt., Dépôt Bn., and retained on Home Service. In the Dépôt Bn. to Dec. 1916; Warwick Detachment, Army Pay Corps, from Jan. 1917 to demobilization. Appointed Lance-Corpl., July 1917; promoted Corpl., Oct. 1917. N.C.O. in charge of Section for Assessing Dependants' Allowances, from Feb. 1918. Demobilized on 14 Mar. 1919. Resumed work at the Press.

Beesley, J. W. (Machine Room, Wharfedale). [Previous Service in the Territorials for eighteen months.] Mobilized with the 4th Oxf. & Bucks L.I. on 4 Aug. 1914. Served in the 1/4th Bn. in England to Mar. 1915, and in France from 30 Mar. to May. Wounded (in the head) in the Second Battle of Ypres (Ploegsteert) on 9 May 1915. In hospital and convalescent in England to 20 Sept.; then with the 3/4th Bn. until discharged, on account of injuries, on 28 Sept. 1916. Resumed work at the Press.

Beesley, R. T. (Bindery, apprentice). Enlisted on 17 Feb. 1917. Served in England in the 13th Roy. Warwick Regt. to 4 Oct. following; then to France in the 15th Hants Regt. Transferred in December to the 1st Hants Regt. Taken prisoner in the Retirement in the following spring, at Monchy (Arras), 28 Mar. 1918. Repatriated on 19 Nov., being at that time in a German hospital, slightly gassed, and in broken health. Subsequently in hospital and convalescent in England. Demobilized on 15 Feb. 1919. Resumed work at the Press.

BEESLEY, W. E. (Stereo and Electro Room, apprentice electrotyper). [Previous Service with the Territorials for nine months.] Mobilized with the 4th Oxf. & Bucks L.I. on 4 Aug. 1914. Served in England in the 1/4th and 2/4th Bns. to Nov. 1915; in the 83rd Provisional Bn. from Nov. 1915 to Jan. 1916; and in the R.D.C. thenceforward to demobilization. Appointed Lance-Corpl. Demobilized on 28 Feb. 1919. Resumed work at the Press (finisher).

BELCHER, H. (Machine Room, wash-house). Enlisted in May 1915 in the 4th Oxf. & Bucks L.I. Served in the 3/4th Bn. in England until transferred to the 2/4th Bn. and sent to France on 24 May 1916. Served thenceforward in France to the end of 1918, taking part in all engagements with the 2/4th Bn. Wounded (left arm) in the Retirement of Mar. 1918. Promoted Corpl. Demobilized on 24 Jan. 1919. Resumed work at the Press.

BELLINGER, L. (Machine Room, feeder, Miehle). [Previous Service in the 4th Oxf. & Bucks L.I. (T.F.) from Nov. 1913.] Mobilized with the 4th Oxf. & Bucks L.I. on 4 Aug. 1914, serving in the 1/4th Bn. and later in the 2/4th. Discharged, on account of ill health, on 4 Aug. 1916. Resumed work at the Press.

BELLINGER, R. C. (Machine Room, apprentice, Wharfedale). Enlisted on 29 Feb. 1916. Served in England with the Queen's Royal West Surrey Regt. to 30 Aug. 1916, and in France with the 6th City of London Regt. from 31 Aug. to 9 Oct. 1916. Wounded (Somme), and suffered loss of right arm. Discharged, on account of injury, on 27 June 1917. Resumed work at the Press (Monotype Casting Room).

BENNETT, R. (Machine Room, compo-house). Enlisted on 28 Jan. 1916. Served in England in the 12th Devon Regt., to 14 June following; and in France in the same unit from 15 June until transferred on 6 Apr. 1917 to the 153rd Labour Coy. Was in France and, afterwards, in Germany to 17 July 1919. Invalided home from Germany with spinal malady. Still under treatment.

BEST, A. E. (Machine Room, feeder, Wharfedale; and wash-house). [Previous Service in the 4th Oxf. & Bucks. L.I., T.F., for seven months.] Mobilized on 4 Aug. 1914 with the 4th Oxf. & Bucks L.I., serving in England successively in the 1/4th Bn. and the 2/4th Bn. to May 1915, and then in the R.F.A. Was in France (R.F.A., 61st Division) from May 1916 to June 1919. Promoted Corpl. and Sergt. Demobilized on 26 June 1919.

† Best, J. T. (Machine Room, feeder, Huber). [Previous Service in the 4th Oxf. & Bucks L.I., T.F., for seven months.] Enlisted in Sept. 1914 in the 4th Oxf. & Bucks L.I. and posted to the 2/4th Bn. Served in England in that unit to 1915, in the 83rd Prov. Bn. 1915–16, in the R.D.C. 1916–17, and in the 24th Cheshire Regt. 1917–18. Died, of pneumonia, on 3 Aug. 1918.

Best, R. E. (Machine Room, feeder, Huber). [Previous Service in the Territorial Force for four years.] Enlisted on 1 May 1915 in the 4th Oxf. & Bucks L.I. Served in England in the 3/4th Bn. to the end of the following January, then in France in the 1/4th Bn. until wounded (thigh, feet, and wrist) on 23 July 1916. After treatment in hospital and period of convalescence was posted to the 3/4th Bn. on 29 June 1917. Drafted again to France, to 1/4th Bn., on 22 July, serving there until 16 Nov. 1917, and afterwards in Italy to Feb. 1919. Engagements: Battle of the Somme, July 1916; Ypres, Oct. 1917; Austrian Offensive, June 1918. Demobilized 18 Feb. 1919, and returned to the Press (Monotype Staff, hand-press).

Best, S. (Night-watchman). [Previous Service in the 4th Bn. Oxfordshire L.I. (Militia).] Enlisted on 30 Mar. 1915 in the 2/4th Oxf. & Bucks L.I. Supernumerary Co. and served in England with that unit to Dec. 1917. Transferred to the R.D.C. and served in France for a short time (Dec. 1917 to Jan. 1918) and then in England to demobilization on 10 Feb. 1919. Resumed duty at the Press.

Biggs, T. A. (Machine Room, Wharfedale). [Previous Service in the 4th Oxf. & Bucks L.I. (T.F.) for four years.] Enlisted on 1 Sept. 1914 in the 4th Oxf. & Bucks L.I. Served in England in the 1/4th and 2/4th Bns., and in France (2/4th Bn.) from 24 May to 23 Dec. 1916, when he was invalided home. In engagements with the 2/4th Bn. in July 1916. Transferred to Labour Corps on 21 July 1917, serving in England until demobilized in Feb. 1919. Resumed work at the Press.

Binder, F. C. (Bindery). [Previous Service in the 1st V.B. Leicester Regt. for four years (covering the Boer War period),

Sergt.] Enlisted on 7 Sept. 1914 in the 4th Oxf. & Bucks L.I. and was posted to the 1/4th Bn. In France with the 1/4th Bn. from 30 May 1915 to 19 Apr. 1917. Was engaged in the Second Battle of Ypres, 1915; Somme, 1916; in the fighting around Peronne in 1917, where he was wounded (for the second time). Returned to England and served in the 4th Res. Bn. Oxf. & Bucks L.I. from 11 June 1917 to demobilization. Promoted Sergt. Demobilized on 17 Jan. 1919. Resumed work at the Press.

BING, A. Y. (Monotype Staff, keyboard). Enlisted on 1 Sept. 1914 in the Oxf. & Bucks L.I. and was posted to the 7th Bn. Served in England to 19 Sept. 1915, in France to Nov. 1915, in Salonika to Sept. 1918, and in Bulgaria to Dec. 1918. Engagements: Capture of Horseshoe Hill, 18 Aug. 1916; Spring Offensive on the Doiran Front, Apr.–May 1917; and the Great Advance, 20 Sept. 1918. Appointed Lance-Sergt. Demobilized on 27 Jan. 1919. Resumed work at the Press.

BISHOP, A. J. (Warehouse). Enlisted on 27 Mar. 1916 in the 4th Oxf. & Bucks L.I., serving in England in the 4th Res. Bn. to 24 July following. Posted to the 1/4th Bn. and served in France from 25 July 1916 to Nov. 1917 (Battle of Somme, Aug. 1916; Peronne, Mar. 1917; Ypres, Aug.–Sept. 1917), and in Italy from Nov. 1917 to Feb. 1919 (Asiago, 15 June 1918; Advance into Austria, 1–3 Nov. 1918). Served subsequently in the 1/6th Gloster Regt. in Albania, Mar.–Apr. 1919, and in Egypt, May–Dec. 1919, and then in the 2/13th London Regt. (Egypt) to Mar. 1920. Demobilized Apr. 1920. Resumed work at the Press.

† BLAKE, J. J. (Bindery). Enlisted on 31 May 1915 in the 4th Oxf. & Bucks L.I. Retained on Home Service throughout. Served for a few months in the 3/4th Bn., and thenceforward in the Labour Corps (attd. Oxf. & Bucks L.I.). Suffered from heart-strain when serving in the West of England in 1916, and again in Northumberland in 1918. Discharged, incapacitated, on 11 October 1918, and died a few days later (21 Oct.) of heart disease.

BOLTON, F. (L.S. Composing Room, apprentice). Enlisted on 16 Feb. 1917. Served in England in the 15th Worcs. Regt. until demobilized on 29 Mar. 1919. Resumed work at the Press.

BOORE, E. (Jobbing Room, compositor). Enlisted on 16 Oct. 1916 in the 1st Garr. Bn. Worcs. Regt. and served in England to the following July. Served in Egypt, in the 1st Garr. Bn. Warwick Regt. from July to Nov. 1917, and in the R.A.M.C. thenceforward to 25 Aug. 1919. Demobilized 8 Sept. 1919. Resumed work at the Press.

† Bowen, A. E. (Monotype Staff, keyboard), had served for ten months with the Press Volunteer Platoon before he enlisted on 26 Mar. 1917 in the 4th Oxf. & Bucks L.I. After a short training in England in the 3/4th Bn. he was posted to the 2/4th Bn. in France on 18 June, and was killed in action at Cambrai on 6 Dec. of the same year.

Bowen, A. J. (Controller's Staff). [Previous Service in the Volunteers (2nd V.B. Oxf. L.I.) and Territorials (4th Oxf. & Bucks L.I.) for thirty years (1884–1914); also in Press Volunteer Platoon (Sergt.) until enlistment.] Enlisted on 3 Dec. 1914 in the Oxf. & Bucks L.I., serving in England successively in the 9th Bn. Oxf. & Bucks. L.I. and in the 36th and 33rd Bns. Training Reserve, in the 280th Infantry Bn., and in the 51st Bn. Hampshire Regt., to Mar. 1919. Served in Germany (British Army of the Rhine) with the 51st Bn. Hampshire Regt. from 18 Mar. to 4 May 1919. Promoted Sergt., C.Q.M.S., R.Q.M.S. Demobilized 9 May 1919. Resumed work at the Press.

Bowen, C. E. (L.S. Composing Rooms, Overseer's Staff). [Previous Service in the Volunteers (2nd V.B. Oxf. L.I.) and in the Territorials (4th Oxf. & Bucks L.I.) for twenty-nine years (1885–1914).] Mobilized with the 4th Oxf. & Bucks L.I. (Platoon Sergt.) on 4 Aug. 1914 and served with the 1/4th Bn. throughout. In England to 29 Mar. 1915, and in France from that date to Apr. 1916. Engaged in trench warfare. Promoted C.Q.M.S. Discharged (termination of engagement) on 17 Apr. 1916, and returned to the Press.

Bowen, W. J. (L.S. Composing Room). [Previous Service in the Volunteers (2nd V.B. Oxf. L.I.) and Territorials (4th Oxf. & Bucks L.I.) for twenty-three years (1888–1911); also in Press Volunteer Platoon (Sergt.) until enlistment.] Enlisted on 20 June 1917 in the R.D.C., serving in England in that corps to Mar. 1918, in the Roy. West Surrey Regt. to 1 June, and then in the 18th Gloster Regt. Served in France and Belgium in the 18th Gloster Regt. from 2 Aug. to 20 Dec. 1918, and in the Labour Corps from 21 Dec. 1918 to demobilization. Was in the Auchy engagement of Oct. 1918. Demobilized on 22 Feb. 1919. Resumed work at the Press.

Bowerman, P. H. (Bindery, apprentice). [Previous Service in the O.V.R. (Band) for a few months.] Enlisted on 11 July 1916 and posted to the 2/7th Durham L.I. To France on 16 Mar. 1917 in the 20th Durham L.I. Wounded at Ypres in the following July—gunshot wounds, necessitating amputation of leg. In hospital and convalescent in England (Lance-Corpl.) until discharged, on account of injuries, on 13 Feb 1919. Resumed work at the Press.

Bowler, A. E. (Collotype Room). [Previous Service in the Oxf. Vol. Regt.] Enlisted in the A.S.C. on 29 Nov. 1915, serving in England to 17 Feb. 1917, and then in Egypt, Palestine, Syria, to 28 May 1919. Engagements: Gaza, Beersheba, Jerusalem, Aleppo. Wounded (in the side) when crossing the Mediterranean, the vessel being torpedoed. Demobilized on 26 June 1919. Resumed work at the Press.

Bowler, A., junior (Controller's Staff). Enlisted on 5 Feb. 1916 in the 2nd Worc. Regt. (Bandsman), and served (Home Service) in the 5th Bn. to 26 Aug. 1917, and then at the Dépôt, Worc. Regt., to July 1919. Returned to the 2nd Bn. on 22 July 1919, and is still serving (Bandsman).

Brewerton, T. F. (L.S. Composing Room, apprentice). Enlisted in the Roy. Navy on 12 Feb. 1915. Served on H.M.S. *Powerful* to June 1915, and then on H.M.S. *Carysfort* to Feb. 1919. H.M.S. *Defiance*, Feb. to June, and in the Caspian Sea (Russia) on H.M.S. *Kruger* from July to Sept. 1919. Engagements: Jutland, May 1916; Zeebrugge, May and Nov. 1917. Rated A.B., Sept. 1916. Now in the Service for twelve years.

Bricknell, W. H. (Bindery). Enlisted on the 7 Sept. 1914 in the 1/4th Oxf. & Bucks L.I. Owing to an accidental injury sustained whilst in training in the 1/4th Bn. he was retained on Home Service throughout, serving successively in the 1/4th, 2/4th, 3/4th, and 83rd Prov. Bns., and in the 2/7th Essex Regt. Discharged, on account of ill health, on 28 Mar. 1917. Resumed work at the Press.

† Brocks, W. A. R. (Machine Room, apprentice, Wharfedale). [Previous Service in the Q.O.O.H. for two years.] Mobilized with the Q.O.O.H. in Aug. 1914. Served in England to Sept., and then in France for two years. In Ireland from Nov. 1916 to Aug. 1917. Then in Egypt in the 3rd Cheshire Regt., and in Palestine (Nov.–Dec. 1917) attd. 16th Devon Regt. Was in engagements in Belgium, France, Egypt, Palestine. Appointed Lance-Corpl. Q.O.O.H.; gazetted

2nd Lieut. Cheshire Regt. Wounded and taken prisoner (misreported killed in action), Dec. 1917; died at Afion, Kara Hissar, Asia Minor, 9 Mar. 1918.

BROGDEN, S. (Warehouse). Enlisted on 29 Mar. 1915 in the 128th H.B., R.G.A., serving in that unit in England for twelve months and in France from 20 Mar. 1916 to 21 Feb. 1919. Engagements: Battle of Messines, 7 June 1917; Third Battle of Ypres, Aug. 1917. Promoted Bdr. Demobilized 22 Feb. 1919. Resumed work at the Press.

BROOKS, F. (Machine Room, feeder, Miehle). Enlisted in Feb. 1917, serving in the 8th Somerset L.I. in England to 25 Sept. 1917 and then in France to 16 Jan. 1918. In engagements at Ypres. Discharged, owing to broken health, on 20 Feb. 1918.

BULLEN, L. (Type Foundry, apprentice). Enlisted on 15 June 1918 in the Oxf. & Bucks L.I., serving in England in the 3rd Bn. to October. In France with the 2nd Bn. (52nd) from 13 Oct. 1918 to Mar. 1919. Re-enlisted.

† BURDEN, A. (L.S. Composing Room). [Previous Service in the 4th Oxf. & Bucks L.I., T.F.] Enlisted in Aug. 1914 in the Oxf. and Bucks L.I. Served in England to December, then posted to the 2nd Bn. (52nd) in France. Was engaged in the Battle of Ypres. Killed in action at Richebourg on 16 May 1915.

BURDEN, H. W. (Bindery). Enlisted on 15 Apr. 1915 in the 4th Oxf. & Bucks L.I., and posted to the 2/4th Bn. Served in England to Mar. 1916, and in France from 7 Mar. to 16 Sept. 1916. In engagements on the Somme, and wounded (gunshot) in left arm. Discharged, on account of impaired health, on 6 Dec. 1917.

BURGESS, F. J. (L.S. Composing Room). [Previous Service in the Press Volunteer Platoon from its formation.] Enlisted on 31 July 1918. Served in No. 3 Port Detachment, Southampton, R.A.F., until demobilized on 27 Feb. 1919. Resumed work at the Press.

BUSHNELL, H. (Bindery, apprentice). Enlisted on 6 Apr. 1918. Served in England in the London Regt. throughout—at first in the 25th Bn. and afterwards in the 10th (Res.) Bn. Demobilized on 4 Feb. 1919. Resumed work at the Press.

BUTCHER, G. W. (Photographic Dept., apprentice). [Previous Service in the 4th Oxf. & Bucks L.I., T.F., for two and a half years.] Mobilized on 4 Aug. 1914 with the 4th Oxf.

& Bucks L.I., serving in England successively in the 1/4th and 2/4th Bns. and in France in the 2/4th Bn. from 24 May 1916 until wounded on 21 Mar. 1918. Was in practically all engagements with the 2/4th Bn. in that period. Promoted Sergt.; Military Medal. Wounded in face—fractured upper jaw—facial disfigurement. Still undergoing plastic surgery, he was released from Army and placed under the Ministry of Pensions in 1921. Resumed work at the Press 3 Oct. 1921.

Cann, J. P. (L.S. Composing Room). [Previous Service in the 2nd (Prince of Wales's) V.B. Devon Regt. for nineteen years.] Enlisted in the R.A.F. on 24 July 1918, serving in England. Demobilized on 4 Jan. 1919. Resumed work at the Press.

Cansdell, T. (Machine Room, Wharfedale). Enlisted on 7 Feb. 1916 in the 8th Wilts Works Coy., serving in England in that unit to 27 May 1917, in the 10th (King's Liverpool) Works Coy. to 30 Aug. 1917, and subsequently in the Labour Corps. Promoted Corpl. Demobilized in Sept. 1919 and returned to the Press for a short time, but broken health disabled him from work until Jan. 1921, when he resumed his former duties at the Press.

Carr, R. (Lithographic Room). Enlisted on 2 Feb. 1915 in the 4th Oxf. & Bucks L.I., serving in England in the 2/4th Bn. to 4 May 1916, and then in the 83rd Prov. Bn. until discharged, on account of ill health, on 25 Oct. 1916. Returned to the Press.

Carter, F. P. (Machine Room, feeder, Miehle). [Previous Service in the 4th Oxf. & Bucks L.I. (T.F.) from 1909.] Mobilized with the 4th Oxf. & Bucks L.I. on 4 Aug. 1914, serving in the 1/4th Bn. in England to 29 Mar. 1915, and then in France until discharged, time-expired, early in 1916. Engaged in trench warfare. Re-enlisted in Aug. 1917, and drafted to the 1/4th Bn. in Italy. In the Asiago fighting and the Austrian Offensive. Promoted Sergt. (in Italy). Demobilized on 3 Mar. 1919. Resumed work at the Press.

Castle, C. S. (L.S. Composing Room). Enlisted in Aug. 1915 in the 4th Oxf. & Bucks L.I. Discharged (under age) in 1916. Re-enlisted later. No further details have been obtained.

Chadder, W. T. (Secretary's Office). Served in the Roy. Fusiliers throughout, enlisting on 6 Dec. 1915, at Oxford. In England in the 29th Bn. to July 1916, and then in France in the 9th Bn. to Nov. 1916, when he was wounded. In

England in the 5th Bn. to Jan. 1917, and again in France, in the 1st Bn., to Aug. 1917, when he was sent home for appendicitis operation. In England in the 5th Bn. to Apr. 1918, and again in France, in the 13th Bn. to Aug. 1918, when he was wounded a second time. Engagements: Somme, 1916; Messines, 1917; Ypres, 1917 and 1918. Demobilized on 10 Apr. 1919. Resumed work at the Press.

† Chapman, F. W. (Monotype Staff, keyboard). Enlisted on 22 Oct. 1915 in the 156th H.B., R.G.A., serving in England first in that unit and then in the 168th H.B. to Aug. 1916. To France in the 168th H.B. on 28 Aug. Transferred to the 136th H.B. in the following month, and to the 128th H.B. in Sept. 1917. Engagements: Vimy Ridge, July 1917; Loos, Aug. 1917; Somme, 21 Mar. 1918. Wounded in head (at Loos), Aug. 1917, and in hand, Sept. 1917. Killed in action on 12 Apr. 1918.

† Chapman, H. S. (L.S. Composing Room, apprentice). [Previous Service in the O.V.R. until enlistment.] Enlisted on 16 Nov. 1916 in the M.G.C. Served in England until 3 Apr. 1917. Crossed to France on that date. Killed in action in the following month, 12 May 1917.

Chapman, R. W. (Assistant Secretary to the Delegates of the Press). Gazetted 2nd Lieut. R.G.A. on 26 Mar. 1915. In England with the 18th H.B. for six months, and then in the Salonika Force from 17 Oct. 1915 to 3 Dec. 1918, in the 18th H.B., the 43rd Siege Battery, and other R.G.A. units. Attained the rank of Temp. Capt. Took part in the engagements of Sept. 1916, 24 Apr. 1917, 7 May 1917, and others on the Doiran front. Demobilized on 3 Mar. 1919. Returned to the Press.

Cherrill, S. G. (L.S. ComposingRoom). Enlisted on 28 Mar. 1917 and posted to the 16th Worc. Regt., serving in England in that unit throughout. Demobilized on 11 Aug. 1919. Resumed work at the Press.

† Clack, W. C. (Machine Room, feeder, Miehle). Enlisted on 14 Sept. 1915 in the R.A.M.C., Field Amb., crossing to France on 23 Oct. 1915. Killed in action on the Hindenburg Line on 13 Apr. 1917.

Claridge, F. J. (Monotype Staff, Casting Room). Enlisted in the Roy. Navy (Boy Tel.) on 3 May 1917. Served in the R.N.B., Shotley, to 28 Jan. 1918, and on H.M.S. *Queen Elizabeth* to 8 Feb. 1919. Afterwards on H.M.S. *Victory*, *Leviathan*, *Royal Sovereign*, and *Renown*. Present at the Surrender of the German Fleet. Still in the Navy, having signed on for twelve years.

Cleaver, A. C. (Type Foundry). [Previous Service in the 2nd V.B. Oxf. L.I. for four years.] Enlisted on 28 Mar. 1917. Posted to the Oxf. & Bucks L.I., serving in England in the 3rd Bn. to the November following. In France in the 2/7th Roy. Warwick Regt. from 9 Nov. 1917 to 18 Aug. 1918 (having been gassed on 8 Aug.), and thenceforward in England. At St. Quentin, 21 Mar. 1918. Discharged, on account of bronchial affection due to gas, on 4 Apr. 1919. Resumed work at the Press.

Cleaver, E. F. (Monotype Staff, keyboard). Enlisted on 22 Oct. 1915 in the 156th H.B., R.G.A., training in that unit until sent abroad. In France in the 116th Siege Battery, R.G.A., from Aug. 1916 to Jan. 1919. Engagements: Somme, 1916; Arras, Apr. 1917; Messines, June 1917; Third Battle of Ypres, July–Nov. 1917; Ypres Retirement, Apr. 1918; Aisne Battle, May 1918; Somme Advance, Aug. 1918; Arras Advance, Sept. 1918; Great Advance (Ypres–Courtrai), Sept.–Nov. 1918. Appointed Lance-Bombardier. Demobilized on 20 Jan. 1919. Resumed work at the Press.

Cleaver, R. A. (L.S. Composing Room, apprentice). [Previous Service in the Territorials for seven months.] Mobilized with the 4th Oxf. & Bucks L.I. on 4 Aug. 1914, serving in England in the 1/4th Bn. and then in the 2/4th Bn. to May 1916, and in France (2/4th Bn.) from that time until wounded (bullet-wound in ankle) and taken prisoner at St. Quentin, Mar. 1918. Engagements: Fromelles, 19 July 1916; Somme, Dec. 1916; Passchendaele, Aug. 1917; Cambrai, Dec. 1917; St. Quentin, Mar. 1918. Returned from Germany in December. Demobilized on 22 Feb. 1919. Resumed work at the Press.

Cleaver, W. E. (Machine Room, Wharfedale). Enlisted on 15 Oct. 1915 in the R.A.O.C. and was sent to France a few days later (30 Oct.), serving continuously thenceforward except for a period in hospital (synovitis, &c.). Demobilized on 16 May 1919. Resumed work at the Press.

Clements, W. G. (Machine Room, apprentice). [Previous Service in the 4th Oxf. & Bucks L.I. (T.) from Nov. 1913.] Mobilized with the 4th Oxf. & Bucks L.I. on 4 Aug. 1914, serving in England in the 1/4th Bn. to Nov., and in the 2/4th Bn. until posted with reinforcements to the 1/4th Bn. in France in June 1915. Served in France to Nov. 1916 and then in Italy until early 1919. Was in all engagements with the 1/4th Bn. after June 1915, receiving a slight gunshot wound in face at Pozières, 23 July 1916. Appointed Lance-Corpl.; received the Military Medal for work on the Asiago. Demobilized 24 Mar. 1919. Resumed work at the Press.

Clifford, F. H. (Bindery). [Previous Service in the Territorials from Apr. 1912.] Mobilized with the 4th Oxf. & Bucks L.I. on 4 Aug. 1914, and served with that unit for a short time; but his health proving unequal to the demands of military service he was discharged, on that ground, on 8 Sept. 1914. Resumed work at the Press.

Clifford, R. A. (Warehouse). Enlisted in Oct. 1916 in the Q.O.O.H., and transferred in the following month to the 2/1st Berks Yeomanry, serving in England to Sept. 1917. In France in the 2nd Bn. Roy. Warwick Regt. from Sept. to Nov. 1917, and in Italy and Austria from that time to May 1919. Transferred then to the 22nd Manchester Regt. and served in Egypt until demobilization. Was in engagements at Passchendaele Ridge (Oct. 1917), on the Italian frontier, and at the crossing of the River Piave (Oct. 1918). Promoted Sergt. Demobilized in Jan. 1920.

Collett, W. G. (Counting House, apprentice; temporarily at Wolvercote Mill, Office). Enlisted on 15 Feb. 1917 in the 2/1st Q.O.O.H., serving in England in that unit to December. Posted to the 2/1st Bucks Bn. in France on 18 Dec. 1917, and transferred to the 2/4th Oxf. & Bucks L.I. in Apr. 1918. Wounded in the Advance on 2 Nov. 1918, and in hospital in England from 11 Nov. (Armistice Day) to Jan. 1919. Served thenceforward in the Res. Bn. in England and in the 52nd Bn. in Ireland until discharged, on account of injuries, in Sept. 1919. Resumed work at the Press.

Collier, L. (Warehouse). Enlisted on 1 Sept. 1914 in the 4th Oxf. & Bucks L.I., serving in the 1/4th Bn. throughout. In England to 29 Mar. 1915, and then in France until wounded in the Battle of the Somme on 23 July 1916, at Pozières. Suffered the loss of a leg, and was discharged 30 May 1917. Resumed work at the Press.

Collins, C. W. (L.S. Composing Room, apprentice). [Previous Service in the Q.O.O.H. for two years.] Mobilized with the Q.O.O.H. on 4 Aug. 1914, serving in England until 19 Sept. 1914, and then in France until the end of 1918. Engagements: First and Second Battles of Ypres (Loos), Sept. 1915; Arras, 1917; Cambrai, Nov. 1917; the Retirement, Mar. 1918; Cambrai, 1918. Demobilized 16 Jan. 1919. Resumed work at the Press.

Cook, E. (Machine Room, Wharfedale). Enlisted in Sept. 1914 in the 4th Oxf. & Bucks L.I., serving in the 1/4th Bn. in England to 29 Mar. 1915, and then in France and later in Italy. Demobilized on 10 Feb. 1919. Resumed work at the Press.

Cook, S. C. (Monotype Staff, Reading Room). Enlisted on 14 Sept. 1914 in the 4th Oxf. & Bucks L.I., serving in the 1/4th Bn. in England to Mar. 1915, and then in France to Dec. 1916. Suffered from heart-strain and returned to England (4th Res. Bn.) until discharged, on account of broken health, on 21 Sept. 1917.

Cooke, F. W. (Machine Room, Wharfedale, apprentice). [Previous Service with the O.V.R., on the East Coast from 27 June to 3 Aug. 1918.] Enlisted on 14 Aug. 1918. Served in the 52nd Devon Regt. (Bugler), in England to 9 Mar. 1919, and afterwards in Germany with the Army of the Rhine. Demobilized in Feb. 1920. Resumed work at the Press.

Cooper, A. B. (Photographic Room). Enlisted on 16 Oct. 1914 in the R.A.M.C., 3rd Wessex Field Amb., and served in England to 1 Feb. 1917. Went abroad with the Advanced Photo. Sect. A.P.S.S., serving in France from 1 Mar. 1917 to 23 Dec. 1918, and then in Germany to 3 Mar. 1919. Appointed Lance-Corpl.; promoted Corpl. Demobilized on 10 Mar. 1919. Resumed work at the Press.

Cooper, E. E. (Machine Room, feeder, Miehle). [Previous Service in the Territorials for four years.] Mobilized with the 4th Oxf. & Bucks L.I. on 4 Aug. 1914. Served in the 1/4th Bn. in England to 29 Mar. 1915, and then in France until discharged, time-expired, on 29 Feb. 1916. Returned to the Press. Re-enlisted on 22 Feb. 1917 in the Royal Navy and served on H.M.S. *Pembroke* to 21 June 1918, and then on H.M.S. *Astraea*, escorting convoys, &c. Was for a short time attached to the Nigerian Marines. German East Africa from Aug. to 1 Dec. 1917, and British West Africa from that time to 11 Nov. 1918. Rated A.B. 21 May 1918. Demobilized on 16 Sept. 1919. Resumed work at the Press.

Cooper, F. W. (Machine Room, Miehle). Enlisted on 29 Mar. 1915 in the R.A.M.C., serving in England successively with the 12th Coy. and the 34th Coy. Appointed Lance-Corpl. Demobilized on 15 Mar. 1919. Resumed work at the Press.

† Cooper, W. F. (Monotype Staff, compositor). Enlisted on 4 June 1915 in the 4th Oxf. & Bucks. L.I. Posted to the

4th Res. Bn. and served in England to Feb. 1916. In France in the 1/4th Bn. from Feb. 1916 to Mar. 1917; in England (3/4th Res. Bn.) to June 1917; and again in France, in the 1/1st Bucks Bn., to 16 Aug. 1917, when he was killed in action in the Third Battle of Ypres.

Copeman, S. (L.S. Composing Room). Enlisted on 1 Sept. 1914. Posted to the 7th Bn. Wilts Regt. and served in England in that unit to October following. Transferred to the 156th H.B., R.G.A., on 1 Nov. 1915. Served in France successively in the 156th and 321st Batteries from 19 June 1916 to 23 June 1919. Engagements: Somme, Passchendaele, Arras, Mons (1918). Appointed A/Sergt. Wounded in leg and shoulder. Demobilized on 25 July 1919. Resumed work at the Press.

Corbey, A. (Stereo and Electro Room, finisher). Enlisted on 18 Sept. 1914 in the 4th Oxf. & Bucks L.I., serving in the 1/4th Bn. in England to 29 Mar. 1915, and then in France to 10 May 1916. Discharged on 23 Aug. 1916, ' no longer physically fit for War service '. Resumed work at the Press.

Corbey, A. V. (Machine Room, Wharfedale). [Previous Service in the Q.O.O.H. for five years.] Enlisted on 1 Sept. 1914 in the 4th Oxf. & Bucks L.I. Served in the 1/4th Bn. in England to 29 Mar. 1915, and in France from that time to 10 Nov. 1917, taking part in all engagements with the 1/4th Bn. in that period. Returned to England (10 Nov. 1917) for six months' rest, under the War Office substitution plans; appointed Bombing Instructor at Reserve Dépôt, and afterwards transferred to Command Dépôt; also on Demobilization Staff. Promoted Corpl. Demobilized on 22 Mar. 1919. Resumed work at the Press.

Cousins, W. G. (Stereo and Electro Room). Enlisted on 11 Aug. 1917 in the R.F.C. (Boy). In Mar. 1918 he was engaged in connexion with bombing operations, North Sea. In France in the R.A.F. from 12 Apr. 1918 to 1 Mar. 1919, and then in Scotland (attd. Roy. Navy) to 10 May 1919. Promoted A.C. 2, Apr. 1919. On 10 May 1919 he was attd. Roy. Navy for service afloat with warships, and is still serving.

Cox, A. C. E. (L.S. Composing Room). Enlisted in Nov. 1915. Served in England in the 2/7th Durham L.I. to Oct. 1917, then for a time in the 29th City of London Regt., and afterwards in the 33rd London Regt. Served in France in the latter unit, attd. No. 2 Coy. A.S.C., 14th Div. Train. Demobilized on 19 Feb. 1919. Resumed work at the Press.

Cox, F. (L.S. Warehouse). Enlisted on 9 July 1917 in the R.A.O.C., remaining on Home Service throughout. Appointed Lance-Corpl. Jan. 1919. Demobilized 31 May 1919.

Cox, H. (Monotype Staff, compositor). Enlisted in Sept. 1914 in the 4th Oxf. & Bucks L.I., serving in England until Nov. 1918, and then in the 11th Royal Sussex Regt. (Corpl.) in France from 13 Nov. 1918 to 4 Mar. 1919. Demobilized on 6 Mar. 1919.

Cox, H. G. (Machine Room, feeder, Huber). Enlisted on 22 Mar. 1916 in the 4th Oxf. & Bucks L.I. Served in France in the 1/4th Bn. (48th Div.) from May 1916 until slightly wounded at Pozières in the following November. In the 4th Res. Bn. (hospital and convalescent), first in England and afterwards in Ireland, from Dec. 1916 to May 1917. Again in France, in the 6th Oxf. & Bucks L.I. (20th Light Div.), from May 1917; was at Ypres (Langemarck) and at Cambrai (Gouzeaucourt), receiving a slight head-wound in the latter engagement. After a few weeks in England (4th Res. Bn., hospital and convalescent), was again in France from early 1918, first in the 2/5th (Notts and Derby) Sherwood Foresters (49th Div.) and afterwards in the 1st Bn. of the same regiment (8th Div.). Engaged in bombing at Oppy Wood; was in the Retirement of Mar. 1918. Demobilized on 19 Jan. 1919. Resumed work at the Press.

Cripps, A. E. (Monotype Staff, compositor). Enlisted on 3 June 1915 in the 4th Oxf. & Bucks L.I. and was posted to the 3/4th Bn. Served in England in that unit to 20 May 1916, and thenceforward in France in the 2/4th Bn. to 19 Jan. 1919. Engagements: Auber's Ridge, 1916; Somme, 1916; Arras (Monchy), 1917; Ypres (Passchendaele Ridge), 1917; Cambrai (Gouzeaucourt), 1917; St. Quentin (Fayet), 1917–18; Cambrai, 1918. Appointed Lance-Corpl. Wounded in thigh (shrapnel) on 19 July 1916 (at Auber's Ridge). Demobilized on 9 Feb. 1919. Resumed work at the Press.

Crook, W. R. (Machine Room). Enlisted on 19 Oct. 1915 in the 4th Oxf. & Bucks L.I., and was posted to the 2/4th Bn. Served in England in that unit to 27 Mar. 1916, in the R.D.C. to 1 June 1918, and in the R.E. to demobilization on 20 June 1919. Resumed work at the Press.

Cummins, A. E. (Jobbing Room, office). Enlisted on 17 Apr. 1918 and posted to the Roy. Warwick Regt., remaining on Home Service to the end of September and crossing to France on 2 Oct. 1918. Demobilized on 8 Sept. 1919. Resumed work at the Press.

Davis, C. J. (Warehouse). [Previous Service in the regulars, 6th Rifle Brigade (Sergt.).] Called up as reservist on the outbreak of war. Served in the 1st (Garr. Bn.) Oxf. & Bucks L.I. (Sergt.) in England to Apr. 1915, and then in India to July 1919. Demobilized on 15 Aug. 1919. Resumed work at the Press (Engineers' Staff).

Deacon, H. A. (Monotype Staff, compositor). [Previous Service in the 4th Oxf. & Bucks L.I., T.F., for five years.] Mobilized with the 4th Oxf. & Bucks L.I. on 4 Aug. 1914, remaining on Home Service—in the 1/4th and 2/4th Bns. to May 1915, in the 83rd Prov. Bn. to Nov. 1916, in the 13th Devon Regt. (Ireland) to Apr. 1918, and thenceforward in the 15th Worc. Regt. Promoted Corpl., Nov. 1914; Sergt., Jan. 1915. Demobilized on 2 Feb. 1919. Resumed work at the Press.

Dixon, S. (L.S. Reading Room). Enlisted on 2 Jan. 1915 in the Roy. Fusiliers, and was posted to the 21st Bn., serving in that unit in England to 14 Nov. 1915, and then in France to 18 May 1916. In England, in the 10th Cadet Bn. from 19 May to 26 Sept. 1916, and in the M.G.C. (2nd Lieut.) to 14 Feb. 1917. In France, with the 5th Brigade Coy., M.G.C., from that date to 14 Nov. 1917. In England, hospital and convalescent (under treatment cutaneous affection contracted in trenches), from Nov. 1917 to Aug. 1918. In France with the 11th Bn. M.G.C. from 28 Aug. to 14 Nov. 1918, and thenceforward on Home Service. Engagements: Albert–Bapaume, Feb.–Mar. 1917; Vimy, first Oppy attack, 10 Apr.–5 May 1917; Final Advance, Arras–Mons, Aug.–11 Nov. 1918. Gazetted 2nd Lieut., 26 Sept. 1916; recommended, Apr. 1917; Lieut., 26 Sept. 1918. Demobilized 5 Apr. 1919. Resumed work at the Press.

Drake, W. F. (Steward of the Press Institute). Enlisted on 4 Sept. 1916 in the Roy. Navy (Officer's Steward). On Home Service throughout. Demobilized on 10 May 1919.

† Draper, W. H. (L.S. Composing Room, apprentice). Enlisted on 14 Sept. 1914 in the 4th Oxf. & Bucks L.I., and served in the 1/4th Bn., crossing to France on 29 Mar. 1915. Appointed Lance-Corpl. Was in various engagements with the battalion up to that of Pozières, where he was killed in action, on 23 July 1916.

Dunning, S. (Machine Room, Wharfedale). Enlisted in Oct. 1915, having then been employed at the Press for about five months. He has not returned to the Press and few details have been obtained. He served first in the 156th H.B., R.G.A., and was at one time serving as Gunner in the 14th S.B., R.G.A., in France. In Jan. 1919 he was in a Military Hospital at Lichfield, recovering from influenza, and was discharged or demobilized shortly afterwards.

East, E. H. (Monotype Staff, Casting Room). Enlisted on 5 Jan. 1916 in the Roy. Navy, serving (Foreign Service) on H.M.S. *Resolution.* Was present at the Surrender of the German Fleet. Still serving.

† Edgington, P. J. (Bindery). Enlisted on 8 Dec. 1916 in the Coldstream Guards. Served in England for a year and was drafted to France on 28 Dec. 1917. He was killed in action near Moyenville, whilst serving with the 1st Bn., on 21 Aug. 1918.

Edmonds, E. (L.S. Composing Room, apprentice). [Previous Service in the 4th Oxf. & Bucks L.I., T.F., for three and a half years.] Enlisted on 5 Aug. 1914 in the 4th Oxf. & Bucks L.I., serving in the 1/4th Bn. in England to 29 Mar. 1915, and then in France until the Battle of the Somme. Was twice wounded. Afterwards on Home Service, first in the 4th Res. Bn., and then attd. 53rd (Y.S.) Roy. Warwick Regt. as bombing instructor. Appointed Lance-Corpl., Nov. 1914; promoted Corpl., Sept. 1915, and Sergt., May 1917. Demobilized on 23 Jan. 1919. Resumed work at the Press.

Edmunds, J. J. (Machine Room, Miehle). [Previous Service in the 2nd (V.B.) Norfolk Regt. for five years.] Enlisted in Oct. 1915 in the A.S.C., serving in England for about three weeks and then in Salonika. Invalided home in Oct. 1916. Subsequently in hospital and convalescent until discharged in Apr. 1917. Resumed work at the Press.

Edwards, F. (L.S. Composing Room, hand-press). Enlisted on 31 May 1915 in the Q.O.O.H. Subsequently transferred to another regiment and served in Egypt and in Mesopotamia; and prior to demobilization was in France. Demobilized on 7 May 1919. Resumed work at the Press. (Now in Canada.)

Eeles, E. J. (Bindery, apprentice). [Previous Service in the 4th Oxf. & Bucks L.I. for five months.] Mobilized with the 4th Oxf. & Bucks L.I. on 4 Aug. 1914, serving in England in the 1/4th Bn. to 2 Nov. and then in the 2/4th Bn. to 1916. In France in the 2/4th Bn. from 24 May to 19 July 1916, when he was wounded (gunshot) in left shoulder at Laventie. After a period of Home Service in the 3/4th Bn. from 20 Sept.

1916, he was posted to the 1/4th Bn. in France, but remained a few days only (11 to 22 Jan. 1917). Returned to England, and served in the 4th Res. Bn. from 11 Mar. 1917 to 10 Feb. 1919. Appointed Lance-Corpl., July 1917. Discharged, disabled and surplus to requirements, 10 Mar. 1919. Resumed work at the Press.

EGGLETON, H. E. (Counting-House). Enlisted on 24 Apr. 1917 in the R.G.A. (Signaller), serving in England to the end of the following March, and in France from 1 Apr. to 9 Nov. 1918. Contracted acute influenza and was in hospital and convalescent in England from that time until demobilized on 25 Jan. 1919. Resumed work at the Press.

ELLIS, R. (Monotype Staff, compositor). Enlisted on 22 May 1916. Served in the Q.O.O.H. in England to 5 June and in Ireland to 6 Dec. Served in France in the 1/4th Oxf. & Bucks L.I. from 6 Dec. 1916 to 22 Nov. 1917, and was then in hospital to the end of that year. Transferred to the Labour Corps and continued foreign service therein from 1 Jan. 1918 to demobilization. Engagements: Peronne, Mar. 1917; Passchendaele, Aug.–Sept. 1917. Demobilized on 22 Mar. 1919. Resumed work at the Press.

FATHERS, E. H. (L.S. Composing Room, apprentice). [Previous Service in the Press Platoon for about six months.] Enlisted on 16 Feb. 1917. After training in England was posted to the 2nd Hants Regt. (Lance-Corpl.) in France in December. Wounded (in leg) in the Retirement of Mar. 1918. Subsequently on Home Service in the 53rd (Y.S.) Bn. Hants Regt. (Corpl.). Demobilized on 26 Jan. 1919. Resumed work at the Press (L.S. Reading Room).

FAULKNER, D. C. (L.S. Composing Room). Enlisted on 23 Oct. 1916 in the Oxf. & Bucks L.I., serving in England to 29 Nov. following. Posted to the 1st Bn. (43rd) and served in India, 3 Mar.–23 Apr. 1917, and in Mesopotamia from 1 May 1917 to 16 Jan. 1919. Engagements included Hit, 26 Feb. and 9 Mar. 1918; and Khan Baghdadieh, 26–27 Mar. 1918. Appointed Lance-Corpl. Demobilized on 17 Apr. 1919. Resumed work at the Press.

FAULKNER, H. C. (Machine Room, counter). Enlisted in Sept. 1916 in the 25th Rifle Bde., remaining on Home Service until drafted to France to the 17th Hants Regt. in Sept. 1918. Subsequently employed in guarding prisoners at a Chinese Detention Camp (in France). Demobilized on 5 May 1919. Resumed work at the Press.

†Fisher, F. C. (L.S. Composing Room, apprentice). [Previous Service in the Q.O.O.H. for two years.] Mobilized with the Q.O.O.H. on 4 Aug. 1914 and served in England (in the 2/1st) for a short time, but was discharged on account of ill health. Returned to the Press. Re-enlisted on 13 Mar. 1915, in the 128th (Oxford) H.B., R.G.A., serving in England to 21 May 1915, and thenceforward in France. He was in various engagements; and it was whilst serving on enemy aircraft observation duty that he received the wounds from which he died a week later, 3 June 1916.

Fisher, V. C. (Engineer's Staff). [Previous Service in the Volunteers for four years.] Enlisted on 2 June 1916 in the R.E., serving therein until 29 July following. After that date he was employed on Munitions until his demobilization on 21 Dec. 1918. Resumed work at the Press.

Foster, A. T. (B.S. Composing Room). [Previous Service in the Volunteers for four and a half years.] Enlisted in July 1916 in the R.F.A., serving in England throughout. Demobilized in October 1919.

Foster, A. W. (Bindery). Enlisted on 24 Mar. 1917 in the R.F.A.; transferred on 28 July to the R.G.A., and served in France from 26 Sept. to 30 Nov. 1917, when his health gave way. Discharged, on account of ill health, on 6 June 1918. Resumed work at the Press.

Foster, C. (Photographic Room). [Previous Service in the Volunteers and Territorials for twenty-one years.] Mobilized with the 4th Oxf. & Bucks L.I. (Sergt.) on 4 Aug. 1914, serving in the 1/4th Bn. in England to 29 Mar. 1915 and then in France until invalided home on 25 Sept. Subsequently on Home Service in the 3/4th Bn. from 10 Oct. 1915 until demobilization. Was engaged in trench warfare (Ploegsteert and Hebuterne). Demobilized on 14 Apr. 1919. Resumed work at the Press.

Foster, C. H. (Machine Room, Wharfedale). Enlisted on 14 Sept. 1914 in the 4th Oxf. & Bucks L.I., serving in the 1/4th Bn. in England to 29 Mar. 1915, and then in France to 27 Aug. 1917. Engagements: Somme Battles, July–Dec. 1916 (capture of Pozières, 19 and 23 July); German retirement from Peronne, 21 Mar., and series of battles Mar.–June 1917; Ypres Battles, July–Aug. 1917. Wounded (gunshot) in right forearm at Le Sars on 28 Nov. 1916, and in left knee at Ypres on 16 Aug. 1917. Discharged, on account of injury to knee, on 2 Mar. 1918. Resumed work at the Press.

Foster, E. (Machine Room, Wharfedale). Enlisted on 5 Dec. 1916 in the R.G.A. Served in England in the R.F.A. to 20 Apr. 1918, and in the R.G.A., Anti-Aircraft Section, thenceforward until demobilized on 23 Feb. 1919. Resumed work at the Press.

Foster, J. (L.S. Composing Room). [Previous Service in Volunteers for three years; in National Reserve for two years.] Enlisted on 10 Nov. 1914 in the R.A.M.C., T., serving in England in that corps continuously to demobilization. Promoted Corpl., 1915; Sergt., 1918; Q.M.S.; W.O. 2nd cl., Jan. 1919. Demobilized on 30 Apr. 1920. Resumed work at the Press.

Franklin, H. E. (Warehouse). Enlisted on 3 Sept. 1914 in the Oxf. & Bucks L.I. Served in the 6th Bn. in England to July 1915, and in France to 14 Sept. 1916, taking part in the Somme and other engagements. Wounded at Guillemont (seven wounds, none very serious), and subsequently on Home Service (Oxf. & Bucks L.I.) from 13 Apr. to 2 July 1917. Then, after a few weeks in the 630th Employment Coy., was transferred to the R.A.M.C., serving in England from 29 Aug. 1917 to 30 Mar. 1918, and thenceforward in France (R.A.M.C.). Demobilized on 1 Feb. 1920. Resumed work at the Press.

Franklin, W. T. H. (Controller's Staff, apprentice). Enlisted on 20 Nov. 1915 in the Roy. Fusiliers. On Home Service in the 29th Bn. to 21 Aug. 1916, and then in the 3rd Seaforth Highlanders until sent abroad. Served in France in the 7th Black Watch, R.H. (Corpl.), from 17 Feb. 1918 to 10 Apr. 1919. Engagements (1918): Cambrai, 21 Mar.; La Bassee, 9 Apr.; Marne, 20 July; Arras, 26 Aug.; Cambrai, 7 Oct. Demobilized on 16 May 1919. Resumed work at the Press.

Frost, F. P. (Machine Room, Plate Stores). Enlisted on 28 Mar. 1917. Served in the A.S.C., M.T., throughout; in England to 14 July, and in Mesopotamia from 18 Aug. 1917 to 17 Jan. 1920, returning via India. Was in several minor engagements: Jebel Hamrin 3–5 Dec. 1917; drive towards Kifri, Kirbuk, Tuz, Apr.–May 1918. Demobilized on 2 Mar. 1920. Resumed work at the Press.

Frost, F. W. (Jobbing Room). [Previous Service in the 2nd V.B. Oxf. & Bucks L.I. for three years.] Enlisted on 14 June 1916 in the Oxf. & Bucks L.I., serving in England in the 3rd Bn. until sent abroad. In France in the 5th Bn. from Mar. to Oct. 1917. Engagements: Arras, in the spring of 1917. Suffered from trench fever. Discharged, unfit for further military service, on 7 Mar. 1918. Resumed work at the Press.

† Fuller, G. H. K. (Monotype Staff, compositor). Enlisted on 31 May 1915 in the Oxf. & Bucks L.I. and served in England (3/4th Bn.) to the following March. In France in the 1/4th Bn. from 10 Mar. 1916. Was in engagements on the Somme, and was killed in action at Thiepval Wood on 16 Aug. 1916.

Gardner, W. H. (Jobbing Room, hand-press). [Previous Service in the Territorials for three years.] Mobilized with the 4th Oxf. & Bucks L.I. on 4 Aug. 1914, serving in the 1/4th Bn. in England to 29 Mar. 1915, and in France from that time to Dec. 1916. On Home Service in the 4th Res. Bn. from 1 Jan. to 6 June 1917. Posted again to the 1/4th Bn. and served in France from June to Nov. 1917 and then in Italy. Was in engagements on the Somme, 1916; Ypres, 1917; and the Austrian Offensive of June 1918, when he was captured by the Austrians and remained in their hands to the end of the year. Demobilized on 2 Mar. 1919. Resumed work at the Press.

Garrett, A. (Bindery). Enlisted on 10 Dec. 1915 and posted to the 2/9th Bn. of the Hants Regt. Served in England to Sept. 1916 (in Cyclist Bn. from 27 July). Posted to the 2/4th Bn. of the same Regt. he served in Palestine from Oct. 1916 to May 1917, and in France from June 1917 until, in Sept. 1918, having contracted muscular rheumatism, he was sent home for medical treatment. Engagements included (Palestine) the capture of Gaza, and (France) Gommecourt Wood. Employed on the purifying of water supply in Palestine. Discharged, on account of rheumatism, on 4 Mar. 1919.

Gass, E. L. (L.S. Reading Room). [Previous Service in the Volunteers and Territorials for twenty-seven years.] Mobilized with the 4th Oxf. & Bucks L.I. (Col.-Sergt.) on 4 Aug. 1914. Served in England throughout: in the 1/4th Bn. to 15 Nov. 1914; 2/4th Bn. to 12 June 1915; 83rd Prov. Bn. to 14 Nov. 1916; 10th Oxf. & Bucks L.I. to 4 July 1917; and in the 2/1st Roy. Wilts Yeom. to 5 Nov. 1917. Transferred on the latter date to Class W (T.F.R.), in order to resume civil occupation at the Press upon urgent War printing. Demobilized on 23 Jan. 1919. Worked for several months in 1919 on the printing staff of the British Delegation to the Peace Conference in Paris. Resumed work at the Press.

†George, C. (Machine Room, Wharfedale). Enlisted on 28 Aug. 1914 in the Oxf. & Bucks L.I., serving in England in the 3rd Bn. to 26 Jan. 1915. In France from that date in the 2nd Bn. (52nd), and, later, for two years travelling on Secret Service. Engagements (1915): La Bassee, 12–16 Mar.; Festubert, Richebourg, Neuve Chapelle, May (reported missing); Loos, Sept. Died, at Prague, on 17 Dec. 1918.

George, F. W. (Machine Room, Wharfedale, apprentice). Enlisted on 16 Feb. 1917. Served in England in the 35th Training Bn. to 26 Apr., and in the 94th Training Bn. to 1 Dec. In France in the 2nd Hants Regt. from Dec. 1917 until wounded in the following September. Engagements: the Retirement, Mar. 1918; the Advance, Aug.–Sept. 1918. Wounded in abdomen and right forearm, 4 Sept. 1918. Discharged, on account of injuries (partial disablement of arm), 14 Feb. 1919. Returned to the Press (Monotype Staff, Reading Room).

Goddard, E. J. (Monotype Staff, compositor). [Previous Service in the Oxf. & Bucks L.I. (Vol. and T.F.) for seven years (stretcher-bearer).] Enlisted on 2 Oct. 1914 in the 1st Sup. Coy. 4th Oxf. & Bucks L.I., serving in England in that unit to the end of Apr. 1916; in the Royal Defence Corps to the following October; and then in the 4th Res. Bn. Oxf. & Bucks L.I. to Jan. 1917. In France in the 2/1st (Bucks Bn.) Oxf. & Bucks L.I. from 28 Jan. to 16 Apr. 1917. Contracted rheumatism in the trenches; the hospital ship *Donegal*, on which he was crossing to England, was torpedoed in the Channel, and he was rescued by the last boat. Afterwards served in England in the Labour Corps. Promoted Corpl. Demobilized in Mar. 1919. Resumed work at the Press.

Goddard, H. R. (L.S. Composing Room). [Previous Service in the Territorials for two years; invalided.] Enlisted on 14 Sept. 1914 in the 4th Oxf. & Bucks L.I., serving for a short time in the 2/4th Bn. Posted to the 1/4th Bn. on 3 Oct. and continued in that unit throughout. In France from 30 Mar. 1915 to 25 Nov. 1917, and then in Italy to Feb. 1919. Engagements: Battles of Somme (1916) and Ypres (1917); the Advance on Trentino (Austria). Appointed Lance-Corpl. Dec. 1914. Demobilized on 12 Feb. 1919. Resumed work at the Press.

Goddard, S. A. W. (Machine Room, Wharfedale, apprentice). Enlisted in Feb. 1917 in the R.G.A. Retained on Home Service throughout: in the R.G.A., Plymouth Defences, from 31 Dec. 1917 to 21 Apr. 1918; in the Cadet School,

R.A.F., from May to Aug.; and in the 8th R.A.F. Cadet Wing from Sept. 1918 until demobilized on 23 Feb. 1919. Resumed work at the Press.

GODDARD, W. H. (Machine Room, Miehle). [Previous Service in the Volunteers for seven years and in the Territorials for four years.] Enlisted on 1 Sept. 1914 in the 4th Oxf. & Bucks L.I., and served with the 1/4th Bn. in England to 29 Mar. 1915; in France to 22 Nov. 1917; and in Italy to the end of Jan. 1919. Engagements: All with the 1/4th Bn., including Somme, July–Sept. 1916; Passchendaele, July–Oct. 1917; Asiago Plateau, June 1918. Appointed Lance-Corpl., Feb. 1915; promoted Corpl., Sept. 1916; Meritorious Service Medal; Mentioned in Dispatches. Demobilized on 8 Feb. 1919. Resumed work at the Press.

GRAY, B. H. (Entry Office). Enlisted on 14 Sept. 1914 in the 4th Oxf. & Bucks L.I., and served in England in the 2/4th Bn. to June 1915; in the 83rd Prov. Bn. to 8 Dec. 1916; and in the 3rd Oxf. & Bucks L.I. until sent abroad. Served in France in the 5th Oxf. & Bucks L.I. from 25 Mar. to 9 June 1917. Engagements: Arras, May 1917. Wounded (gunshot) in left arm and shoulder, and gassed. Discharged, on account of injuries, on 16 Oct. 1917. Resumed work at the Press.

GRAY, B. R. (Lithographic Room). Enlisted on 10 May 1915 in the 4th Oxf. & Bucks L.I. and served in England successively in the 3/4th Bn. (to 3 July), in the 2/4th Bn. (to 5 Dec.), in the 83rd Prov. Bn. (to 11 Aug. 1916), in the 4th Res. Bn. Oxf. & Bucks L.I. (to 28 Mar. 1918), and in the 2/1st Q.O.O.H. to July. Served in the 2/24th London Regt. ('Queen's'), in France from 9 July to 21 Sept. 1918, and in Belgium to 13 June 1919. Engaged in the Final Advance, July–Nov. 1918. Appointed Lance-Corpl., Aug. 1917; promoted Corpl., Sept. 1918. Demobilized on 17 July 1919, and re-enlisted in the Oxf. & Bucks L.I. (Regulars).

†GREEN, G. W. (L.S. Composing Room, apprentice). Enlisted on 31 Aug. 1914 in the 4th Oxf. & Bucks L.I., serving in the 1/4th Bn. in England to 29 Mar. 1915, and in France from that time until Nov. 1916. Under treatment for trench fever, and in England in the 4th Res. Bn. from Jan. to Mar. 1917; and in France in the 5th Bn. from that date. Appointed Lance-Corpl. Engagements: Somme, July 1916; Arras, May 1917. Killed in action in the latter engagement on 3 May 1917.

Green, W. A. (Machine Room, Wharfedale). Enlisted on 19 Sept. 1914 in the 4th Oxf. & Bucks L.I., serving in England in the 2/4th Bn. until 17 Mar. 1915. Discharged on that date, on medical grounds. Resumed work at the Press.

Green, W. E. (L.S. Reading Room). Enlisted on 31 Jan. 1917, and served in England in the Devon Regt. for a short time. Went to France on 27 Feb. 1917. From 1 Aug. 1917 to 14 Jan. 1918 was in hospital and convalescent (trench fever). Thenceforward in the 374th (H.S.) Lab. Coy. until demobilized on 20 Jan. 1919. Resumed work at the Press.

Griffin, H. G. F. (Lithographic Room). [Previous Service in the Volunteers for two years and in the Territorials for three years.] Mobilized with the 4th Oxf. and Bucks L.I. on 4 Aug. 1914, serving in England in the 1/4th Bn. to 29 Mar. 1915. In France in the 48th Div. Cyclist Coy. from that time to 26 June 1916, and then in England in the 3rd Line Cyclist Coy. to 12 Dec. Again in France, from 12 Dec. 1916, in the L.N. Lancs Regt.—in the 10th Bn. to 21 Mar. 1917, and thenceforward in the 1/5th Bn. Engagements: Second Battle of Ypres, 20 May 1915; Arras, 9 May 1917; Passchendaele Ridge, 1917; Oeustauerne; St. Quentin, 21 Mar. 1918; Riencourt, Sept. 1918; Cambrai, until 10 Oct. 1918; Moevres, Proville, Lille, Oct. 1918; Pont à Chin, 11 Nov. 1918. Promoted Sergt. Was wounded in face, arms, and legs by German stick bomb on 11 May 1917. Demobilized on 21 Feb. 1919.

Griffin, L. R. (Monotype Staff, apprentice). [Previous Service in the Territorials from 8 Oct. 1908.] Mobilized with the 4th Oxf. & Bucks L.I. (Sig. Corpl.) on 4 Aug. 1914, serving in the 1/4th Bn. in England to 29 Mar. 1915, and in France to June 1917. Again in England, in the 21st O.C.B. from July to Oct.; posted to the 4th Roy. Berks Regt. (2nd Lt.) on 31 Oct., serving with that battalion in England to 23 May 1918, and then proceeding to join the 2/4th Bn. in France. R.A.F. Navigation Officer in England from Aug. 1918 onward. Engagements: Trenches, Ploegsteert, 1915, and Hebuterne, 1915–16; Somme, 1916; German Retreat, 1917; Merville, 1918. Promoted Sig. Sergt., 6 Aug. 1914; gazetted 2nd Lt. Roy. Berks Regt., 31 Oct. 1917; secd. 2nd Lt. Navigation Wireless, R.A.F., 9 Nov. 1918; gazetted Lt., 1 May 1919; transferred from Roy. Berks Regt. to Oxf. & Bucks L.I. (T.), 6 July 1920. Military Medal (3 June 1916) for work on 18 Oct. 1915. Demobilized on 2 Sept. 1919. Resumed work at the Press.

Grundy, H. C. (Jobbing Room, compositor). [Previous Service in the 2nd V.B. Oxf. L.I. for four years.] Enlisted in Aug. 1916 in the Cambridgeshire Regt., and served in England to June 1917. In France and Belgium in the 1/6th Gloster Regt. from that month to the following October. Engagements (chiefly in the Third Battle of Ypres, also on the Somme): St. Julien, Steenbeck, 16 Aug.; Passchendaele, 9 and 10 Oct. Wounded in the latter engagement, gunshot wounds in thigh and stomach. Discharged on account of injuries, Apr. 1918. Resumed work at the Press.

† Gulliver, F. J. (Type Foundry). Enlisted on 7 Sept. 1914 in the 4th Oxf. & Bucks L.I. Served in France, in the 2/4th Bn., from 24 May 1916, taking part in various engagements with that unit. Killed in action at Ablaincourt, in the German retreat from the Somme, on Good Friday, 6 Apr. 1917.

Gurden, G. (B.S. Composing Room, apprentice). Enlisted about the end of Aug. 1914 in the Roy. Marines (as regular) and served therein through the War, but no details have been obtained. He was serving on H.M.S. *Royal Sovereign* when he obtained his discharge from the Forces to engage in agriculture in Devon.

Hadley, A. J. S. (L.S. Reading Room). [Previous Service in the Volunteers for four years.] Enlisted on 2 Oct. 1914 in the 1st Sup. Coy., 4th (T.) Oxf. & Bucks L.I. and served in England in the National Reserve to 2 Oct. 1916, and then in the 4th Res. Bn. Oxf. & Bucks L.I. to Dec. 1917. In France in the 2/1st Bucks Bn. Oxf. & Bucks L.I. from that time until wounded at St. Quentin on 25 Mar. 1918. After a period in hospital he was retained on Home Service, and later on Demobilization Staff. Promoted Sergt. Demobilized in the autumn of 1919.

Hadley, G. E. (Collotype Room). Enlisted in the A.S.C. on 11 Nov. 1915, serving in England for a few days only; in France from 25 Nov. 1915 to 7 Feb. 1919. Promoted Corpl. Demobilized on 10 Feb. 1919.

Hainge, A. (Monotype Staff, compositor). Enlisted on 1 Sept. 1914. Served in the 7th Wilts Regt. throughout—in England to 12 Sept. 1915; in France to 10 Nov. 1915; in Salonika to 8 June 1918; and again in France to 4 Oct. 1918, when he was wounded (gunshot) in head and leg at Cambrai. Engagements: Loos, Nov. 1915; Doiran (Salonika), 1917; Cambrai, 1918. Discharged, on account of injuries, on 11 Dec. 1918.

Hall, F. J. (Machine Room, feeder, Miehle). [Previous Service in the 4th Oxf. & Bucks L.I. (T.F.) for seven years.] Mobilized with the 4th Oxf. & Bucks L.I. on 4 Aug. 1914, serving in the 1/4th Bn. in England to 29 Mar. 1915 and in France from that date until discharged, time-expired, early in 1916. Worked for a time on munitions (Banbury). Re-enlisted in the R.G.A., serving in England. Transferred to the 12th Devonshire Regt. and was sent to France in Apr. 1917. Wounded (slightly) and sent home for treatment, afterwards returning to France in the Chinese Labour Corps (Corpl.). Demobilized in Feb. 1919.

Hall, W. (Machine Room, feeder, Miehle). Enlisted in Feb. 1917. In training in the 53rd (Y.S., T.R.B.) Roy. Warwick Regt. until the spring of 1918, and then drafted to France to the 15th Essex Regt. Later in 90th Labour Coy. Sustained injury (thumb) whilst serving with a working party on 1 Nov., and subsequently in hospital and convalescent. Demobilized in Feb. 1919. Resumed work at the Press.

Hallett, E. J. (Machine Room, Miehle). [Previous Service in Volunteers for three years.] Enlisted on 10 Nov. 1915. Served in the 14th Worc. Regt. throughout—in England to 20 June 1916, and then in France and Belgium to 16 Feb. 1919. Engagements: Beaumont Hamel (Nov. 1916), the Ancre, Somme (First and Second Battles), Passchendaele, Arras, Cambrai (Advance and Retirement). Promoted Sergt. Demobilized on 16 Mar. 1919. Resumed work at the Press.

Handy, C. (Machine Room, wash-house). Enlisted on 10 Feb. 1915 in the 2/4th Oxf. & Bucks L.I., being discharged, on medical grounds, a few weeks later—22 May 1915.

Harris, A. (Stereo and Electro Room). Served in the Sherwood Foresters and on Home Service throughout, being commissioned temp. 2nd Lieut. on 7 Apr. 1915, and transferred to the 4th Bn. (Special Reserve) on 18 Oct. 1916; Lieut. 1 July 1917; Acting Captain (Adjutant) 3 Aug. 1917. Relinquished Acting Captain (Adjutant) in Oct. 1919 and was demobilized in the following month. Relinquished commission and granted rank of Captain, 1 Apr. 1920.

Harris, E. H. (L.S. Composing Room, apprentice). Enlisted in the 2/4th Oxf. & Bucks L.I. on 15 Sept. 1914, serving in England to 24 May 1916, and then in France to Apr. 1918. Wounded at Marcelcave, bullet wound in right thigh, on 28 Mar. 1918. On Home Service in the 4th Res. Bn., July,

Aug., and from that time to demobilization in No. 5 R.A.F. Cadet Wing. Engagements: Somme, Nov. 1916; St. Quentin, Apr. 1917 and Mar. 1918; Arras, May 1917; Ypres (Passchendaele Ridge), Aug. 1917; Cambrai, Nov. 1917. Appointed Lance-Corpl. Demobilized on 3 Mar. 1919. Resumed work at the Press.

Harris, F. J. (L.S. Composing Room, apprentice). Mobilized with the 4th Oxf. & Bucks L.I. on 4 Aug. 1914. Served in the 1/4th Bn. in England to 29 Mar. 1915, and in France until 1 July 1916, and was in all engagements with the battalion during that period. Returned to England owing to failing health, and was subsequently employed on Home Service successively in the 3/4th Oxf. & Bucks, 5th Norfolks, and the 257th Coy. R.D.C. (Southampton). Demobilized early in Jan. 1919. Resumed work at the Press.

Harris, H. C. (L.S. Composing Room). Enlisted in the 4th Oxf. & Bucks L.I. on 31 Aug. 1914, and served in the 1/4th Bn. throughout: in England to 26 June 1915; in France to 20 Nov. 1917; and in Italy to 22 Feb. 1919. Engagements: Somme, 1916; Third Battle of Ypres, 1917; Austrian offensive, 1918. Appointed Lance-Corpl.; Military Medal (for work on 10 Sept. 1918). Wounded, slightly, at Pozières, July 1916. Demobilized on 3 Mar. 1919. Resumed work at the Press.

Harrison, A. J. (L.S. Reading Room). Enlisted in the 156th H.B., R.G.A., on 26 Oct. 1915. In hospital, with acute cerebro-spinal meningitis, from 22 Mar. to Nov. 1916. Thenceforward retained on Home Service, at the R.G.A. Dépôt, Woolwich. Promoted Sergt. Demobilized on 26 Jan. 1919. Resumed work at the Press.

Harrowell, W. W. (Lithographic Room). Enlisted on 25 July 1916. Posted to R.E. Signal Dépôt, Dunstable (Pioneer). Remustered Sapper 22 Aug. 1917. Appointed A/Lance-Corpl. (Army Signal School, Dunstable) 12 Mar. 1918; A/2 Corpl. 2 Sept. 1918 (employed in Drawing Office); A/Corpl. 13 Feb. 1919. Demobilized 14 May 1919.

Hearne, W. C. (Machine Room, feeder, Miehle). Enlisted on 5 Oct. 1918 and posted to the 52nd Bn. Roy. Warwick Regt. for training. Served in the Army of Occupation, Germany (Lance-Corpl.). Demobilized 18 Feb. 1920.

Heath, F. W. (Machine Room, Huber). [Previous Service in the Territorials for two years.] Enlisted, 13 May 1918, in the R.A.M.C., and served in the 302nd Field Amb. until demobilized on 21 Feb. 1919. Resumed work at the Press.

Higgins, J. C. (Warehouse). Enlisted in Nov. 1916 in the Roy. Wilts Yeom., serving in England first in that unit and afterwards in the 2nd Devon Hussars. Drafted to France to the 11th Leicester Regt. Served in France also in the 8th Leicesters, and was in that unit when wounded at the Second Battle of Ypres on 4 Oct. 1917. After a period of hospital and convalescence in England in the 2/4th Leicesters he was transferred to the Machine Gun Corps and posted to the 200th M.G.C. in France. Engagements included Ypres and Auber's Ridge. Demobilized in May 1919.

† Hiles, A. (L.S. Reading Room). [Previous Service in the Territorials for about a year.] Mobilized with the 4th Oxf. & Bucks L.I., and served with the 1/4th Bn. until taken ill in the following January. Died of pneumonia, 24 Jan. 1915.

† Hill, H. G. (Monotype Staff, keyboard). Enlisted on 18 Jan. 1915 in the 4th Oxf. & Bucks L.I., serving in the 1/4th Bn. Proceeded to France on 6 Feb. 1916. Killed in action on 19 Apr. 1917.

Hine, A. J. (Monotype Staff, compositor). [Previous Service in the Territorials, four and a half years.] Mobilized with the 4th Oxf. & Bucks L.I. on 4 Aug. 1914; discharged, on medical grounds, on 4 Sept. Re-enlisted on 26 Oct. 1916, serving in England in the 2/5th Bedford Regt. to 14 Jan. 1918, and in the 11th Bedford Regt. to the following June. In France and Belgium in the 12th Norfolk Yeom. from 13 June 1918 to 24 Mar. 1919. Demobilized on 25 Mar. 1919. Resumed work at the Press.

Hine, G. (Machine Room, Wharfedale, apprentice). Enlisted on 19 Sept. 1914 in the 4th Oxf. & Bucks L.I., and served with the 2/4th Bn. in England to 24 May 1916, and in France until taken prisoner by the Germans on 27 Mar. 1918 (released 7 Dec.). Engagements: Somme, 19 July 1916 and Mar. 1917; Ypres, 22 Aug. and 10 Sept. 1917. Appointed Lance-Corpl., 28 Aug. 1917. Demobilized on 16 Mar. 1919. Resumed work at the Press.

Hine, G. E. (Machine Room, Wharfedale, apprentice). [Previous Service in the 4th Oxf. & Bucks L.I. for about four years.] Mobilized with the 4th Oxf. & Bucks L.I. (Bandsman) on 4 Aug. 1914. Served in the 1/4th Bn. in England to the end of Mar. 1915, in France to Nov. 1917, and then in Italy to Feb. 1919. Was in all engagements with the 1/4th Bn. to the Hebuterne period; afterwards with the 48th Divisional Band until the Division was sent to Italy; and then in the 48th Div. 'Curios'. Demobilized on 23 Feb. 1919. Resumed work at the Press.

Hine, P. J. (Monotype Staff, compositor). Enlisted on 10 Nov. 1915 in the 30th Labour Coy., A.S.C., serving in England to 6 Dec. 1915, and thenceforward in France; transferred to the 712th Labour Coy. on 28 Jan. 1918. Demobilized on 26 Jan. 1919. Resumed work at the Press.

Hine, W. T. (Machine Room, Miehle). Enlisted on 20 Oct. 1915 in the A.S.C., serving in England to 14 Nov. following, and in Salonika to 18 Mar. 1919. Appointed Lance-Corpl. Demobilized on 1 Apr. 1919. Resumed work at the Press.

Hodgkins, C. H. (Jobbing Room). Enlisted on 19 May 1915 in the R.A.M.C. and served in Oxford war hospitals until demobilization on 20 Aug. 1919. Promoted Sergt. Resumed work at the Press.

Holt, G. E. C. (Monotype Staff, compositor; temporarily in Entry Office). Enlisted on 21 Nov. 1914 in the 4th Oxf. and Bucks L.I., and served in England in the 2/4th Bn. to 26 June following. In Belgium in the 1st Entrenching Bn. from June to Nov. 1915, and in France in the 1/4th Oxf. & Bucks L.I. to July 1916. Wounded at the Battle of the Somme in July 1916, multiple shrapnel wounds in right leg and arm, and shattered ankle. Under surgical treatment to March following; in the 4th Res. Bn. Oxf. & Bucks L.I. (pending discharge), Mar.–Apr. 1917; and discharged, on account of injuries, on 28 Apr. 1917. Returned to the Press (Reading Room).

Holt, W. (Machine Room, feeder, Miehle). Enlisted in the later months of the War, namely in June 1918. He served in the Army of Occupation, Germany, and later in Ireland in the 1st Oxf. & Bucks L.I. Demobilized on 3 Mar. 1921.

Hopcraft, F. (Photographic Room, apprentice). Enlisted on 23 Jan. 1918 in the 3rd Oxf. & Bucks L.I., serving in England in that unit to November, and in France in the Roy. Bucks Hussars from 23 Nov. 1918 until demobilization on 4 Feb. 1919. Resumed work at the Press.

Hope, G. H. H. (Machine Room, platens, apprentice). [Previous Service in the 4th Oxf. & Bucks L.I. from 1912.] Mobilized with the 4th Oxf. & Bucks L.I. on 4 Aug. 1914, serving in England in the 1/4th Bn. to Mar. 1915, and then in the 2/4th Bn. To France in the 2/4th Bn. in June 1916. Appointed Lance-Corpl. In all engagements with the battalion until wounded at Ypres in Aug. 1917. After a period (hospital and convalescence) in the 3/4th Bn., qualified as Instructor in Bombing and Bayonet Fighting and was attached to the 53rd (Y.S., T.R.B.) Roy. Warwick Regt. Subsequently served in Germany with the Army of the Rhine. Demobilized on 27 Apr. 1919. Resumed work of the Press.

Horwood, F. (Bindery). Enlisted on 31 Aug. 1916. Served in the 2/5th Bedford Regt., in England throughout. Transferred to Class W Reserve, 17 Feb. 1917. Demobilized on 10 Jan. 1919. Resumed work at the Press.

Howard, G. H. (Warehouse). Enlisted on 12 Sept. 1916 in the 4th Oxf. & Bucks L.I., serving in England in the 4th Res. Bn. Discharged on 6 Dec. 1917, ' no longer physically fit for War service '.

Howes, M. J. (Collotype Room). Enlisted on 12 April 1915 in the 4th Oxf. & Bucks L.I., serving in England in the 4th Res. Bn. to 24 Dec. 1916, and in France in the 2/4th Bn. from 25 Dec. 1916 to 12 Mar. following; subsequently under medical treatment until discharge. Engagements: Ablaincourt Sector. Promoted Corpl., 5 May 1917. Discharged, on account of ill-health, on 2 Oct. 1917. Resumed work at the Press.

Howkins, A. H. (Warehouse). [Previous Service in the 2nd V.B. Oxf. L.I. for three years.] Enlisted in the R.A.M.C. on 6 Aug. 1914, and served in England in the 10th Coy. R.A.M.C. throughout (Sergt.). Operating theatre attendant, four years. Engaged in surgical operations by candle-light on P.O. Navy, amputation of leg and excision of kidney, during Gotha Air Raid on Chatham. Contracted sepsis in the hand (1914) whilst dressing wounds. Demobilized on 18 Aug. 1919. Resumed work at the Press.

Howkins, J. L. (Warehouse). Enlisted on 31 May 1916 in the R.G.A. Retained on Home Service throughout. Demobilized on 24 Aug. 1919.

Howkins, J. W. (Bindery). Enlisted on 21 May 1916 in the 11th S.B., R.G.A., serving in that unit in England to Oct. 1916 and then in France until wounded (shrapnel wound in arm) on 21 July 1917. In England, hospital and convalescent, until early in 1918, then sent to France to the 301st S.B. Was in all engagements with each battery whilst abroad. Demobilized on 29 Jan. 1919. Resumed work at the Press.

† Howkins, W. J. (Controller's Staff). Enlisted in the 4th Oxf. & Bucks L.I. in Aug. 1914, serving in the 1/4th Bn. in England to Mar. 1915, and thenceforward in France. Appointed Lance-Corpl. Killed in action at Hebuterne on 31 Dec. 1915.

Hoy, C. D. (Machine Room, Wharfedale). Enlisted on 5 Sept. 1914 in the 4th Oxf. & Bucks L.I., serving in the 1/4th Bn. until discharged, on medical grounds, on 26 Feb. 1915.

Hunt, W. C. (Secretary's Office). Enlisted in the R.F.A. on 31 Aug. 1914, and served in England in B. Battery, 84th Bde., R.F.A., to 24 July 1915. In France in the same Battery (18th Division) to Nov. 1915, in the 3rd Field Survey Coy., R.E., to Feb. 1917, and attached H.Q. 17th Corps R.A. (preparing barrage maps in view of the Arras battle of Mar. 1918) to May 1918. Invalided home, suffering from trench fever, on 4 June 1918. Engagements: Trench warfare on the Somme and in the Arras sector. In the Retirement in Mar. 1918, went back with the 13th Squadron R.A.F., having been temporarily lent to that Squadron at the time. Appointed A/Bdr. in R.F.A.; 2nd Corpl., R.E.; 2nd class Signaller; 1st class Observer. Demobilized on 19 Mar. 1919. Resumed work at the Press.

Hutchins, C. F. (Monotype Staff, keyboard, apprentice). Enlisted on 21 Oct. 1915 in the 4th Oxf. & Bucks L.I., serving in England in the 3/4th Bn. to 16 Jan. and then in the 2/4th Bn. to 24 May 1916. In France and Belgium in the 2/4th Bn. from that date to 31 Aug. 1917, when he was wounded (in knee) at Passchendaele Ridge. After a period of Home Service in the 4th Res. Bn. he served again in France in the 11th Queen's Roy. West Surrey Regt. from 29 Mar. 1918 to 2 Jan., and in Germany from 3 Jan. to 16 Feb. 1919. Engagements: Somme, 1916; Arras (Monchy) and Ypres (Passchendaele Ridge), 1917; Commines, Courtrai, Scheldt, 1918. Promoted Sergt., 10 Mar. 1918. Demobilized on 22 Feb. 1919. Resumed work at the Press.

Hymers, F. W. (L.S. Reading Room). [Previous Service in the 2nd Roy. Fusiliers for four years.] Enlisted in the A.S.C. in Sept. 1915, serving in England to 30 Oct. following, and in France to May 1916. Promoted Corpl. Discharged, on account of rheumatism, July 1916. Resumed work at the Press.

Isaac, F. J. (Monotype Staff, compositor). Enlisted on 2 June 1915 in the Roy. Berks Regt., serving in that regiment throughout; in England in the 3rd Bn. to 23 Oct. 1916, in France in the 2/4th Bn. from that date to 31 Dec. following. Engagements: Somme, Nov. 1916. In England from 1 Jan. 1917, under medical treatment. Discharged, on account of broken health, on 9 Jan. 1918. Resumed work at the Press.

Jacob, F. C. (Machine Room, apprentice). Enlisted on 14 Sept. 1917. Posted to a Training Reserve Bn., and served in England to 31 Mar. following. In France in the Roy. Inniskilling Fusiliers from 1 April to 20 June 1918, and thenceforward in the Roy. Seaforth Highlanders. Was engaged in the fighting at Cambrai, 25 Sept. 1918. Demobilized 4 Feb. 1919. Resumed work at the Press.

Jacob, W. T. (Monotype Staff, keyboard, apprentice). Enlisted on 16 Sept. 1914 in the 4th Oxf. & Bucks L.I., serving in England in the 2/4th Bn. to 6 June 1915, and then in the 3/4th Bn. In France in the 6th Roy. Berks Regt. from 3 Mar. 1917. Wounded in right shoulder on 12 Oct. at Passchendaele Ridge, and gassed (mustard) on 17 Nov. near Houthulst Forest. After a period of hospital and convalescence, was again on Home Service, in the 4th Roy. Berks Regt., from 2 Mar. to 29 June 1918; and thenceforward in Italy in the 48th Bn. M.G.C. Engagements: Poelcapelle; Passchendaele Ridge, Oct. 1917; Third Battle of Ypres, Nov. 1917. Demobilized on 8 Feb. 1919. Resumed work at the Press.

Jacobs, C. F. (L.S. Store Room, apprentice). [Previous Service in the Q.O.O.H. for two years.] Mobilized with the Q.O.O.H. on 4 Aug. 1914, serving in England until 19 Sept. 1914, and then in France until 24 May 1919. Was engaged in the First and Second Battles of Ypres (Loos), Sept. 1915; Arras, Apr. 1917; Cambrai, Nov. 1917; the Retirement, Mar. 1918; Cambrai, 1918 (wounded in arm and thigh). Promoted Sergt. Demobilized on 31 May 1919. Resumed work at the Press.

† Jago, E. L. (Secretary's Office). Enlisted on 22 Oct. 1917. Posted to a Young Soldiers Training Bn. Proceeded to France on 3 May 1918, and joined the 2/8th Worc. Regt. on 7 May. Wounded (in head) whilst the battalion was holding front-line trenches in the Lys salient on 10 July 1918, and died before reaching the dressing station.

Janaway, A. P. (Bindery, apprentice). Enlisted on the 20 Jan. 1916 in the 3rd Res. Bn. Oxf. & Bucks L.I. Served with that unit (later as Gymnastic Instructor) until drafted to the 1st Roy. Berks Regt. (Corpl.) in France in Feb. 1918. Was engaged in the Retirement in the following month; and in the Great Offensive until seriously wounded between Arras and Albert (Monchy). Subsequently in hospital (France and England) until demobilized (from hospital) on 5 Jan. 1919. Resumed work at the Press.

Janaway, W. P. (Monotype Staff, reader). Enlisted on 29 Aug. 1916. Served in England in the Cambs Regt. to 11 Mar. following, and in the Devon Regt. to 14 June. In France in the 180th Lab. Coy. from 15 June 1917 to 12 Feb. 1919. Demobilized on 3 Mar. 1919. Resumed work at the Press.

Jaycock, P. W. (Machine Room, feeder, Miehle). [Previous Service in the 4th Oxf. & Bucks L.I. (T.F.) from Nov. 1913.] Mobilized with the 4th Oxf. & Bucks L.I. on 4 Aug. 1914, serving in England in the 1/4th and 2/4th Bns., and in France in the 2/4th Bn. from 24 May to 21 July 1916. Invalided home and served for a time in the 3/4th Bn. Afterwards transferred to the Labour Corps. Served in the Labour Corps in France from 13 Aug. 1918 until demobilization, 2 Mar. 1919. Resumed work at the Press.

Jeffs, R. L. (Bindery). Enlisted in July 1917, serving in the Labour Corps in England and in France and Germany (Army of Occupation). Demobilized in Nov. 1919.

Johnson, C. T. (Machine Room, Wharfedale). Enlisted on 28 Feb. 1916. Served in England in the 11th East Surrey Regt. to 15 Mar., and subsequently in the 2/5th Norfolk Regt. Proceeded to France on 28 Aug. 1916 with the 1/5th West Riding Regt. Posted to the 1/7th Bn. on 1 Feb. 1918. Engagements: Somme, Sept. 1916; Nieuport, Aug. 1917; Passchendaele Ridge, 7 Oct. 1917. Taken prisoner on 14 Apr. 1918; repatriated 14 Dec., and employed at the Dépôt West Riding Regt. from that time to demobilization on 25 Aug. 1919.

Johnson, R. (Jobbing Room). Served in England in the R.A.F. (Pte., 2nd class) from enlistment on 24 July 1918 to demobilization on 10 Jan. 1919. Resumed work at the Press.

† Jones, D. S. (Monotype Staff, compositor). Enlisted in Sept. 1914 in the 4th Oxf. & Bucks L.I., serving in the

1/4th Bn. In England to 29 Mar. 1915, and thenceforward in France. Promoted Corpl. Killed in action (Battle of the Somme) at Pozières on 23 July 1916.

† Jones, R. G. (Monotype Staff, compositor). Enlisted on 2 Nov. 1915 in the Oxf. & Bucks L.I., and served in England in the 3rd Bn. to Jan. 1917. In France in the 6th Bn. (Lance-Sergt.) from 2 Jan. to 15 Nov. 1917. His health gave way, and from that time onward he was in hospitals and under medical treatment in England for gastric disability (incurable). Discharged from the Army, on that account, on 19 Feb. 1918, remaining under medical care (Ministry of Pensions) until he died, in the Radcliffe Infirmary, on 17 Feb. 1920.

Jones, W. (Warehouse). Enlisted on 31 Aug. 1915 in the 3rd Oxf. & Bucks L.I. Served in that unit in England to Sept. 1916, and in the 2/4th Bn. in France from that time to demobilization on 9 Jan. 1919. Resumed work at the Press.

Judd, R. E. (Bindery Office). [Previous Service for some months in the Press Platoon, O.V.R.] Enlisted on 11 May 1916 in the 4th Oxf. & Bucks L.I. and served in England in the 3/4th Bn. to Oct. 1917. In France in the 1/4th Bn. from 10 Oct. to 27 Nov. 1917; and in Italy in the R.E. from 29 Nov. 1917 onward. Appointed Lance-Corpl.; Signals Instructor. Demobilized on 7 Sept. 1919.

Judge, S. E. (Machine Room, Wharfedale, apprentice). [Previous Service in the 4th Oxf. & Bucks L.I. (T.F.) for four years.] Mobilized with the 4th Oxf. & Bucks L.I. on 4 Aug. 1914, serving in the 1/4th Bn. To France on 29 Mar. 1915, and in all engagements with the battalion until the Battle of the Somme (Le Sars, 6 Nov. 1916), where he sustained several wounds. In hospital and convalescent in the 3rd Res. Bn. for a year. Drafted to the 2/4th Bn. in France in Mar. 1918 (Signaller). Appointed Lance-Corpl., 1918. Demobilized at end of Feb. 1919. Resumed work at the Press.

Jupp, H. (L.S. Composing Room, apprentice). Enlisted on 16 Sept. 1914 in the 4th Oxf. & Bucks L.I., serving in England in the 2/4th Bn. to October, in the 1/4th Bn. to 28 Feb. 1915, and again in the 2/4th Bn. from 1 Mar. 1915 to May 1916. In France in the 2/4th Bn. from May 1916 to Aug. 1917. Wounded at Passchendaele Ridge on 21 Aug. (bullet-wound in left shoulder and lung, shrapnel wounds in groin). Subsequently in England, in hospital; and then in the 52nd Roy. Warwick Regt. to demobilization. Engagements: Auber's Ridge, July 1916; Somme, 1916–17; Arras, Apr. 1917; Ypres, Aug. 1917. Promoted Corpl.; Instructor. Demobilized on 9 Feb. 1919. Resumed work at the Press.

KEEP, G. P. (Bindery Office, apprentice). Enlisted on 30 Aug. 1916 in the Oxf. & Bucks L.I., and served in England in the 3rd Bn. to the following March. In France in the 2nd Bn. from 16 Mar. to 30 May 1917. Again in England (in hospital) in the 3rd Bn. to December. Returned to France to the 6th Bn. on 13 Dec. 1917. Posted to the 2/4th Bn. on 15 Feb. 1918. In Palestine from 30 May 1919 to October, and afterwards in Cairo. Engagements: St. Quentin, Mar. 1918. Promoted Sergt. Demobilized in Dec. 1919. Resumed work at the Press (Controller's Staff).

† KENCH, P. C. E. (Warehouse). Enlisted on 17 May 1915 in the 4th Oxf. & Bucks L.I., serving in England in the 2/4th Bn. Posted to the 1/4th Bn. in France on 6 Feb. 1916. Wounded in action on 13 June following and sent back to England. To France again on 6 Apr. 1917; posted to the 6th Bn. on 7 Sept. Reported missing a fortnight later; presumed killed on or about 20 Sept. 1917.

† KERRY, F. J. (Bindery). Enlisted on 31 May 1915 in the 4th Oxf. & Bucks L.I., serving in England in the 3/4th Bn. until July 1916, and in France in the 1/4th Bn. from that month to Oct. 1917. After a period in hospital and of convalescence in England, he returned to France (12th London Regt.) on 7 Sept. 1918, and was killed in action on the Somme a few days later, 18 Sept. 1918.

KETTLE, H. (Stereo and Electro Room, finisher). Enlisted in Mar. 1917. Served in the Labour Corps in England and overseas. Demobilized on 21 Jan. 1919. Resumed work at the Press.

KILBEE, G. E. (Brewer Street Warehouse). Enlisted on 9 Sept. 1914 in the Oxf. & Bucks L.I., serving in the 8th Bn. throughout. In England to 17 Sept. 1915; in France from 18 Sept. to 18 Nov. 1915; in Salonika from 25 Nov. 1915, to 7 Nov. 1918; and in Bulgaria from that time to 1 Apr. 1919. Engagements: Doiran, 24–25 Apr. and 8–9 May 1917; the advance into Bulgaria, 1918. Demobilized on 3 June 1919.

KIMBER, H. (Warehouse). Served in the Royal Navy from enlistment on 2 Nov. 1915 to demobilization on 16 May 1919. A.B. Engagements: Cattegat, 25 Oct. 1917; Heligoland, 17 Nov. 1917. Resumed work at the Press.

† KIMBER, R. J. (Machine Room, feeder, Miehle). Enlisted on 2 Apr. 1917. Served in England in the 95th Training Res. Bn. for a brief period. Died, at Tidworth Hospital, of cerebro-spinal fever, on 11 May 1917.

KISLINGBURY, E. G. (Monotype Staff, Casting Room). Enlisted on 19 Jan. 1915 in the 4th Oxf. & Bucks L.I., serving in the 2/4th Bn. in England to 24 May 1916, and then in France until wounded (by gunshot, in back and left lung) on the Somme on 19 July 1916. After a period in hospital and on Home Service in the 3rd Res. Bn., served in Mesopotamia in the 2nd Northumberland Fusiliers from 20 July 1917 to 1 May 1919. Engagements: Battle of the Somme, 19 July 1916. Demobilized on 2 June 1919. Resumed work at the Press.

KISLINGBURY, L. A. (L.S. Composing Room, apprentice). Enlisted on 7 Feb. 1917. Posted to the 1/7th Devonshire Regt. Transferred to the Labour Corps and served in the 41st Labour Coy. in England to 10 June 1919, and then in Germany (Army of Occupation). Demobilized in Nov. 1919. Resumed work at the Press.

KISLINGBURY, W. (Monotype Staff, Casting Room). Enlisted on 14 Sept. 1914 in the 4th Oxf. & Bucks L.I., serving in the 2/4th Bn. in England to 24 May 1916 and then in France until wounded (in the leg) in the July following. After a period in hospital and on Home Service in the 3rd Res. Bn. (29 Sept. 1916 to 2 Feb. 1917) he was posted again to France to the Bucks Bn. about Easter, and served in that unit in France to 29 Nov. 1917 and in Italy from that time onward. Engagements: Ypres, 20 Aug. 1917; Austrian offensive, 15 July 1918. Demobilized 30 Apr. 1919. Resumed work at the Press.

† KITCHEN, A. W. (Machine Room, feeder, Miehle). Enlisted on 11 Oct. 1916 in the Oxf. & Bucks L.I., serving in England in the 4th Res. Bn. to 1 Mar. 1917, when he was one of a draft sent to reinforce the 1/4th Bn. in France. He was in engagements at Bullecourt on 23 Apr. and 3 May. Reported missing; presumed to have been killed on 3 May 1917.

† KITCHEN, C. J. (Machine Room and wash-house). [Previous Service in the 4th Oxf. & Bucks L.I. (T.F.) from May 1914.] Mobilized with the 4th Oxf. & Bucks L.I. on 4 Aug. 1914. Served in England in the 1/4th Bn. Proceeded to France on 28 June 1915, and to the Front with No. 1 Entrenching Bn. a month later. Rejoined the 1/4th Bn. in the

field on 7 Oct. 1915, and was wounded in action five days later. He was killed in action at Hermies (Lance-Corpl., 1/4th Bn.) on 21 May 1917.

KNAPP, R. (Machine Room, feeder, Huber). [Previous Service in the Territorials from Feb. 1910.] Mobilized with the 4th Oxf. & Bucks L.I. on 4 Aug. 1914, serving in the 1/4th Bn. in England to 29 Mar. 1915, and then in France to 28 Feb. 1916. Appointed Lance-Corpl., June 1915. Discharged, time-expired, on 29 Feb. Re-enlisted on 4 Aug. 1916 in the 1/5th Queen's Roy. West Surrey Regt., serving in that unit in England to 21 June 1917, and in India and Turkey to 12 Apr. 1919. Demobilized on 13 May 1919. Resumed work at the Press.

LAPWORTH, G. H. (Bindery). [Previous Service in the Territorials for four years.] Mobilized with the 4th Oxf. & Bucks L.I. on 4 Aug. 1914, serving in the 1/4th Bn. in England to 29 Mar. 1915, and in France from 30 Mar. 1915 to 17 July 1917. Suffered from diphtheria (also 'trench feet'), and was thenceforward retained on Home Service, 4th Res. Bn., Sergt. Bombing Instructor. Engagements: Second Battle of Ypres, Ploegsteert region, Apr. 1915; Somme Battle, July 1916; and the fighting in the Peronne region, early 1917. Promoted Sergt. Demobilized on 17 Jan. 1919. Resumed work at the Press.

LAPWORTH, H. J. (Jobbing Room). [Previous Service in the Territorials for seven years.] Mobilized with the 4th Oxf. & Bucks L.I. on 4 Aug. 1914, serving in England in the 1/4th Bn. and also in the 9th Bn. to Dec. 1916. In France in the 8th Devon Regt. from that time to Nov. 1917, and then in Italy to Feb. 1919. Engagements: Attacks on Ecoust, 2 Apr. 1917; Bullecourt, 9 May 1917; Passchendaele Ridge, 4 Oct. 1917; Gheluvelt, 26 Oct. 1917; Asiago Plateau, May 1918; Piave River, 27 Oct. 1918. Appointed A/Corpl., 5 Dec. 1916. Wounded (shell) in shoulder at Bullecourt, 9 May 1917. Demobilized on 2 Mar. 1919. Resumed work at the Press.

LAPWORTH, J. H. (Jobbing Room, apprentice). [Previous Service in the Territorials from 6 Feb. 1914.] Mobilized with the 4th Oxf. & Bucks L.I. on 4 Aug. 1914, serving in England in the 2/4th Bn. to 12 Dec. 1915. In France in the 2/1st Bucks Bn. from 14 Dec. 1915 to 25 Mar. 1916. Suffering from trench feet he was sent to England, remaining on Home Service in the 6th Bn. to 20 Dec. 1917. Returned to France in the 5th Bn. on Christmas Day 1917. Gassed and taken prisoner at St. Quentin, 23 Mar. 1918; repatriated 12 Nov. (day following Armistice). Engagements: Somme, 1916; Ypres, 1917; St. Quentin, 1918. Demobilized on 7 Mar. 1919. Resumed work at the Press.

LEATHERBY, J. W. (Photographic Room). Served in the Oxf. & Bucks L.I. from enlistment on 23 Mar. 1916, to the November following. Transferred to the Photo Sect. A.P.S.S., and served in France from Dec. 1916 to Jan. 1919. Appointed Lance-Corpl., Oxf. & Bucks L.I.; promoted Sergt., Photo. Sect. Demobilized on 1 Feb. 1919.

LEWIS, R. G. (Bindery). [Previous Service in the Volunteers and Territorials for nine years.] Mobilized with the 4th Oxf. & Bucks L.I. on 4 Aug. 1914, serving in England successively in the 1/4th Bn. to 29 Oct. 1914, in the 2/4th Bn. to 20 Nov. 1915, and in the 3/4th Bn. to 6 Aug. 1917. Then in France in the 1/4th Bn. to 22 Nov. 1917, and thenceforward in Italy. Engagements: Ypres; Asiago. Promoted Sergt.; Musketry Instructor. Demobilized on 28 Feb. 1919. Resumed work at the Press.

†LINES, P. G. (Monotype Staff, compositor). Enlisted in Nov. 1915 in the 4th Oxf. & Bucks L.I., serving in the 2/4th Bn. in England and crossing to France in that unit on 24 May 1916. He was wounded at Laventie in the following month (28 June), in the battalion's first bombing raid, and died three days later, 1 July 1916.

LONG, A. (Warehouse). Enlisted as Aircraft Hand in the R.A.F. on 17 June 1918, serving in England from that date until demobilized on 27 Apr. 1919.

LONGFORD, E. (Machine Room, feeder, Miehle). [Previous Service in the V.T.C.] Enlisted on 27 Apr. 1917. Served in England in the 92nd Training Res. Bn. to 17 May, in the 93rd Training Res. Bn. to 4 Sept., and in the 52nd Hants Regt. to 30 Mar. 1918. In France in the 15th Hants Regt. from 1 Apr. 1918, and later in Germany, in the Army of the Rhine. Wounded (shrapnel) in neck on 2 Nov. 1918. Demobilized on 19 Oct. 1919.

LOUCH, H. H. (Machine Room, Wharfedale, apprentice). Enlisted on 9 Sept. 1914. Served in the Royal Fusiliers throughout; in the ranks in the 11th Bn. and 17th Bn. (Lance-Corpl.) in England and France, and as 2nd Lieut. in the 6th Bn. from 28 Mar. 1917. Lieut., 13 Feb. 1919. Demobilized on 16 Jan. 1920. Relinquished his commission, retaining the rank of Lieut., 1 Mar. 1920.

LUDLOW, F. (L.S. Composing Room). [Previous Service in the 1st Devon and Somerset R.E. (Vol.) for eleven years.] Enlisted on 2 Oct. 1914 in the 1st Sup. Coy. 4th Oxf. & Bucks L.I., serving in England in that Coy. to 29 Apr. 1916, and thenceforward in the 258th Protection Coy., R.D.C. Appointed Lance-Corpl. Demobilized on 28 Apr. 1919. Resumed work at the Press.

MANKELOW, F. (Monotype Staff, compositor). Enlisted on 30 Nov. 1916 in the A.S.C. (M.T.), serving in England to 26 June following, and then successively in Salonika, Serbia, Bulgaria, to 10 Mar. 1919, and in Russia to 29 Oct. Demobilized on 24 Nov. 1919. Resumed work at the Press.

MANN, F. (L.S. Composing Room). Enlisted on 16 July 1916 in the Roy. Berks Regt., serving in England for a month and then in France from 18 Aug. 1916 to 27 Jan. 1917. Contracted influenza and neurasthenia, and, after a further period of Home Service, was discharged, on medical grounds, on 22 Feb. 1918. Resumed work at the Press.

†MARGETTS, A. C. (Monotype Staff, keyboard). Enlisted in the 4th Oxf. & Bucks L.I. in Sept. 1914, serving in the 1/4th Bn. in England to Mar. 1915, and then in France until wounded (in foot and face) on the Somme in July 1916. In the 3/4th Bn. in England from 23 July to Christmas Day 1916, and thenceforward in France in the 2/4th Bn. Engagements: Somme, Ypres, and others. Appointed Lance-Corpl., Apr. 1916; promoted Corpl., May 1916. Reported missing 22 Aug. 1917; presumed killed in action, date uncertain.

MARGETTS, F. C. (L.S. Composing Room, apprentice). Enlisted on 4 June 1917. Served in England in the D.C.L.I. (with an interval in the Roy. Warwick Regt.) to the following February. In France in the 7th D.C.L.I. from Feb. 1918 to Feb. 1919. In India and Mesopotamia in the 2nd D.C.L.I. for two years. Demobilized in Mar. 1921. Resumed work at the Press.

MARTIN, J. F. (Bindery). Enlisted on 19 Nov. 1915 in the A.S.C., serving in England to 10 Jan. following, and thenceforward in France (on L. of C.). Promoted Corpl. Demobilized at end of Feb. 1919. Resumed work at the Press.

MASTERS, E. S. (Monotype Staff, compositor, apprentice). [Previous Service in the Territorials for one year and eight months.] Mobilized with the 4th Oxf. & Bucks L.I. on 4 Aug. 1914, serving in the 1/4th Bn. in England to 29 Mar.

1915, and then in France to 12 July 1916. Wounded (on the Somme) in face, arm, and legs, by shrapnel, in July 1916. In the 4th Res. Bn. on Home Service to 30 Mar. 1917, then returned to France in the 2nd Wilts Regt. Taken prisoner in the Retirement of Mar. 1918; in Germany from 21 Mar. to 31 Dec. Other engagements: Somme, 1916; Ypres, 1917. Demobilized on 15 Apr. 1919. Resumed work at the Press.

Masters, F. J. (Stereo and Electro Room, apprentice). [Previous Service in the Territorials for two years.] Mobilized with the 4th Oxf. & Bucks L.I. on 4 Aug. 1914, serving in England in the 1/4th Bn. to 2 Nov., and in the 2/4th Bn. from that date. In France (2/4th Bn.) from 25 May 1916 until taken prisoner at St. Quentin on 21 Mar. 1918. Repatriated at end of year. Engagements: Ypres, Arras, Cambrai, St. Quentin. Demobilized on 26 Mar. 1919. Resumed work at the Press.

Masters, W. H. (Machine Room, feeder, Miehle). Mobilized with the 4th Oxf. & Bucks L.I. on 4 Aug. 1914, serving in the 1/4th Bn. in England to 29 Mar. 1915 and then in France to Nov. 1917; thenceforward in Italy in the Labour Corps. Was in practically all engagements with the 1/4th Bn. in France. Appointed Lance-Corpl.; promoted Corpl.; awarded the Meritorious Service Medal. Demobilized on 25 Feb. 1919. Resumed work at the Press.

Mayo, R. J. (L.S. Composing Room, hand-press). Enlisted on 28 Oct. 1916 in the 10th Oxf. & Bucks L.I., serving in England to June 1917. In France in Bucks Bn. from that time until wounded (gunshot) in right hand at Ypres on 22 Aug. 1917. After a period of hospital treatment in England, returned to France in Roy. Berks. Regt. on 3 Aug. 1918. Gassed at Throne Wood in the following month. Demobilized on 3 Jan. 1919. Resumed work at the Press.

McGregor, A. W. (Machine Room, Wharfedale). Enlisted on 11 May 1917 in the R.A.M.C., serving in England to October and then in France. Invalided home from France on 4 Dec. In hospital and convalescent to Feb. 1918, and afterwards on Home Service until demobilized on 4 July 1919. Resumed work at the Press.

McKenzie, J. (Machine Room, Huber). Enlisted in Oct. 1915 in the A.S.C., and was sent to Salonika in the following month. Returned to England about the end of 1917 and was subsequently retained on Home Service until demobilized in Mar. 1918. Resumed work at the Press.

MERRITT, D. C. (Machine Room, feeder, Miehle). Enlisted on 6 Apr. 1915 in the 4th Oxf. & Bucks L.I., serving in England in the 3/4th Bn. to June, and then in the 4th Worc. Regt. to 4 July. In Gallipoli in the 4th Worc. Regt. from 21 July to 6 Aug. Wounded on that date at Achi-Baba, gunshot wounds in right hand, left arm, and left leg. Discharged, on account of wounds, on 21 Oct. 1916.

†MILLER, H. (Machine Room, Wharfedale). Enlisted on 15 Nov. 1915 in the 4th Oxf. & Bucks L.I., serving in the 2/4th Bn. in England to the following May, and in France from 25 May 1916. Was engaged in sniping. Met with an accident (fractured tibia) on 1 Feb. 1917 and was in hospital in England from 6 Feb. Died, from the effects of the injury, on 18 Feb. 1917.

MITCHELL, A. (Monotype Staff, Casting Room). Enlisted on 3 May 1915 in the 4th Oxf. & Bucks L.I., serving in England to 1 Feb. 1916. In France from 1 Feb. to 24 July 1916, and thenceforward in Mesopotamia. Engagements: Somme offensive; Khan Baghdadieh, Mar. 1918. Wounded in back (shrapnel). Demobilized on 21 Mar. 1919.

MORSE, E. (Warehouse). [Previous Service in the Territorials, 1908–13.] Enlisted on 25 Oct. 1916 in the 4th Roy. Berks Regt. and served in England in that unit throughout. Demobilized on 15 Feb. 1919. Resumed work at the Press.

MOSS, A. (Machine Room, counter). Enlisted on 1 Jan. 1918. Served in England in the 36th Training Res. Bn. to 8 Mar. 1918, in the 18th Sect. R.A.O.C. to July 1919, and attd. Tank Corps from that time to demobilization on 13 Sept. 1919. Resumed work at the Press.

MOSS, P. L. (Stereo and Electro Room, apprentice). [Previous Service in the Territorials for one year.] Enlisted on 5 Aug. 1914 in the 4th Oxf. & Bucks L.I., serving in England successively in the 1/4th Bn. and the 2/4th Bn. to 24 May 1916; and in France in the 2/4th Bn. from that date to Sept. 1918. Subsequently on Home Service (Didcot, &c.). Engagements: Somme, Ypres, St. Quentin. Appointments and promotions: in England—Lance-Corpl., Corpl.; in France—Lance-Sergt., Sergt., C.Q.M.S., Coy. Sergt.-Major. Wounded twice, slightly; gassed twice. Demobilized on 25 Feb. 1919.

MOTT, R. (L.S. Composing Room, apprentice). Enlisted on 17 Sept. 1914 in the 4th Oxf. & Bucks L.I., and served in

England in the 2/4th Bn.; posted to the 83rd Prov. Bn., and subsequently to the 157th T.F. Dépôt. Demobilized on 16 June 1919. Resumed work at the Press.

NASH, W. J. (Lithographic Room). Enlisted on 1 Sept. 1914 in the 4th Oxf. & Bucks L.I., remaining on Home Service throughout, successively in the 1/4th Oxf. & Bucks L.I., in the Devon Regt., and in the R.A.F. Demobilized on 5 Feb. 1919.

NEW, R. H. (Controller's Staff). [Previous Service for a few months in the Press Volunteer Platoon.] Enlisted on 1 May 1917 in the A.S.C., M.T., serving in England to 10 Oct., and thenceforward in East Africa (Lindi district and Dar-es-Salaam) to 12 Mar. 1919. Twice in hospital with malarial fever. Demobilized on 16 May 1919. Resumed work at the Press (now on Secretary's Staff).

NORTH, J. A. (Machine Room, feeder, Miehle). Enlisted on 22 Oct. 1915 in the A.S.C. Served in Salonika from the following month (15 Nov.) to 15 Jan. 1918. Contracted malarial fever. On returning to England he was transferred to the A.S.C., M.T., and retained on Home Service. Engagement: Serbian Retreat, 27 Dec. 1915. Demobilized on 21 Feb. 1919. Resumed work at the Press.

NURSER, E. T. (Controller's Office, B.S., apprentice). Enlisted on 14 Sept. 1914 in the 2/4th Oxf. & Bucks L.I., and crossed to France with the 1/4th Bn. on 29 Mar. 1915. Wounded on the Somme (attack on Pozières) in July 1916, right ear, right hand and knee. In England (in hospital and convalescent) in the 3/4th Bn. from 27 July 1916. Returned to France on 10 Sept. 1917 to the 1/4th Bn., but being then unequal to front-line duty was for about two months attd. Labour Corps. In Italy with the 1/4th Bn. from 1 Feb. 1918 to 1 Mar. 1919. Engagements: Somme, July 1916; Austrian Offensive, 15 June 1918. Demobilized, 1 Apr. 1919. Resumed work at the Press (Machine Room, office).

PANTING, A. W. (L.S. Composing Room, apprentice). [Previous Service in the Press Volunteer Platoon.] Enlisted on 9 May 1917. Served in England in the 34th Training Res. Bn. and in the 51st Hants Regt. to the end of the following March. In France in the 2/4th Hants Regt. from 1 Apr. to 21 Dec. 1918, and afterwards in Germany to 25 Jan. 1919. Engagements (1918): Second Battle of the Marne, July; capture of Havrincourt (12 Sept.), Marcoing (28 Sept.), Solesmes (20 Oct.). One wound. Demobilized on 1 Feb. 1919. Resumed work at the Press.

† Panting, E. F. (Counting House, apprentice). [Previous Service in the Territorials from March 1914.] Mobilized with the 4th Oxf. & Bucks L.I. on 4 Aug. 1914, serving in the 1/4th Bn. to the end of Feb. 1915 (Writtle). Transferred to the 2/4th Bn., serving for a short time at Leafield Wireless Station; but his health was failing, and as no improvement was manifested he was discharged early in 1916. In quest of health he tried motoring, and also took a sea voyage, but without avail. He died, of tuberculosis, on 6 June 1917.

Parker, C. G. (Machine Room, Wharfedale). Enlisted in the 4th Oxf. & Bucks L.I. on 23 Jan. 1915, serving in England. Discharged on 14 Mar. 1916, 'no longer physically fit for War service'. Resumed work at the Press.

Parmenter, C. (L.S. Composing Room, apprentice). Enlisted on 15 Sept. 1914 and was posted to the 4th (Res.) Bn. Oxf. & Bucks L.I. Transferred to the R.E. and posted to the 3/2nd South Midland Field Coy. (Sapper) on 7 May 1915. Was employed on Home Service throughout. Demobilized (5th Res. Bn., Christchurch, A/Lance-Corpl.) on 9 May 1919.

† Partridge, H. E. (Machine Room, Wharfedale). [Previous Service in Volunteers and Territorials for twelve years.] Mobilized with the 4th Oxf. & Bucks L.I. on 4 Aug. 1914, serving in the 1/4th Bn. in England to 29 Mar. 1915, and in France from that time. Killed by an explosion (a grenade falling into the ammunition-box in a bay of the breastwork) in the Second Battle of Ypres (Ploegsteert), on 9 May 1915.

Payne, H. C. (Strong Room). Enlisted in Mar. 1915, serving in the 3rd Seaforth Highlanders in England and in India and Mesopotamia. Invalided home, suffering from malaria. Rejoined the 3rd Seaforths in Feb. 1917, and was retained on Home Service until demobilized early in 1919.

Payne, W. H. (Lithographic Room). [Previous Service in the Territorials for three years.] Mobilized with the 4th Oxf. & Bucks L.I. (Bugler) on 4 Aug. 1914, serving in the 1/4th Bn. throughout. In England to 29 Mar. 1915; in Belgium from that date to 27 June 1915, and afterwards in France. In Italy from 18 Nov. 1917 to 31 Mar. 1919. Engagements: Second and Third Battles of Ypres; Somme; Peronne; and (Italy) Asiago Plateau. Promoted Corpl.-Bugler. Demobilized on 1 May 1919.

Penny, C. A. (Warehouse). Enlisted on 24 Feb. 1917. Served in the 3rd Hants Labour Coy. in England to 16 Mar. following, and thenceforward in France. Demobilized on 6 Mar. 1919.

Perry, L. L. (L.S. Reading Room). Enlisted on 1 Mar. 1916 in the Somerset L.I. Served in England with 13th Roy. Warwick Regt. to July; in the 33rd Training Res. Bn. to Dec. 1916; in the Labour Corps to Dec. 1918, and from that time, in the Dispersal Unit, Fovant. Appointed Lance-Corpl. Demobilized on 2 Sept. 1919. Resumed work at the Press.

Phelps, J. F. (Photographic Room, apprentice). Enlisted on 20 Feb. 1915 in the R.A.M.C., serving in England in No. 48 Coy. throughout. Promoted Corpl., 9 Nov. 1915; Sergt., 11 May 1916; Staff Sergt., 11 Dec. 1917; C.Q.M.S., 16 Jan. 1919. Officially mentioned for services rendered, 1915–1919. Demobilized on 29 Apr. 1919. Resumed work at the Press.

Phipps, G. (Brewer Street Warehouse). [Previous Service in the Regular Army, in India; and in the National Reserve.] Called up as National Reservist in Nov. 1914. Retained on Home Service, and was with the 83rd Prov. Bn. when discharged, in 1917, on account of deafness. Resumed work at the Press (Brewer Street).

Pimm, J. T. (Jobbing Room, compositor, apprentice). Enlisted on 26 Feb. 1917 in the Roy. Berks Regt., serving in England in the 4th Res. Bn. until the New Year. In France in the 2nd Bn. from 5 Jan. 1918, until slightly wounded and taken prisoner in the Champagne district on 27 May following. Repatriated on 1 Jan. 1919, afterwards serving in Ireland in the 2nd Bn. from March onward. Engagements (1918): Retirement, 22 Mar.; Amiens, Apr.; Champagne, 27 May. Signaller. Demobilized on 19 Sept. 1919. Resumed work at the Press.

Piper, C. D. (L.S. Composing Room, apprentice). Enlisted in the 4th Oxf. & Bucks L.I. on 31 Aug. 1914, serving in the 1/4th Bn. in England until 29 Mar. 1915, and thenceforward in France and Belgium until discharged, time-expired, in May 1916. Re-enlisted in the following month, serving in 3/4th Bn. to Oct., and afterwards in France in the 2/1st Bucks Bn. to Dec. Again in England in the 3/4th Bn. to Feb. 1917; and in the 5th O.C.B. (at St. John's, Cambridge) from Feb. to May. In France in the 13th Rifle Brigade from July to Oct. Gassed on 2 Oct. and subsequently in England (hospital and convalescent) to Mar. 1918, and in the 5th Rifle Brigade to July. Back in France in the 13th Rifle Brigade from Aug. (wounded in that month) to Oct. In England (Instructor in Bombing) in the 51st (Y.S.) Rifle

Brigade from Oct. 1918 to Mar. 1919. In Germany (and Russia, Danzig, Jan. 1920) in the 53rd Rifle Brigade from Mar. 1919 to Mar. 1920. Engagements: Hill 60, Somme (1916); Messines; Passchendaele Ridge. Promoted Corpl.; Gazetted 2nd Lt.; Lt., Rifle Brigade. Demobilized on 6 Mar. 1920. Resumed work at the Press.

Powell, A. A. E. (Bindery, apprentice). Enlisted on 20 Oct. 1916 in the A.S.C., M.T., and was transferred early in the following year to the Tank Corps. Served in France in the 8th Bn. Tank Corps, from 1917. Demobilized in Feb. 1919.

Price, F. (L.S. messenger). [Previous Service in the 4th Bn. (Militia) Oxfordshire L.I. for ten years.] Called up as Corpl. in the National Reserve on 14 Aug. 1914, serving in England in the R.D.C. (Corpl.) for over three years. Discharged (in consequence of injuries received in an accident whilst handling stores) on 18 Feb. 1918. Resumed work at the Press.

† Price, O. O. (Photographic Room). [Previous Service in the Territorials for three years.] Mobilized with the 4th Oxf. & Bucks L.I. (Corpl.) on 4 Aug. 1914, serving in the 1/4th Bn. in England to 29 Mar. 1915, and thenceforward in France. Engagements: Somme, July 1916. Promoted Sergt. Killed in action at Pozières on 23 July 1916.

Prosser, A. (Examination Paper Room). Enlisted on 1 Oct. 1917 in No. 2 Cadet Coy., A.S.C., H.T. & S., serving in England in that Coy. to the end of the year, and at the Supply Personnel Dépôt from 13 Feb. to 29 June 1918. In France from that date, at No. 2 Base M.T. Dépôt (364th Coy., A.S.C., M.T.), to Nov. 1919. Demobilized on 10 Nov. 1919. Returned to the Press.

Putnam, S. G. W. (Machine Room, feeder, Wharfedale). Enlisted on 10 Feb. 1915 in the 4th Oxf. & Bucks L.I., serving in the 2/4th Bn. Crossed to France in the 2/4th Bn. on 24 May 1916, and served there in that unit until 17 Aug. following. Transferred to Army Reserve a week later, and employed (in England) on munitions. Recalled to military service on 8 May 1917, and served (in France) to 20 Jan. 1919. Re-enlisted next day, at Zons on the Rhine, for a period of three years. Proceeded with the 1st Bn. Oxf. & Bucks L.I. to North Russia (Gen. Ironside's Expedition to Archangel), 12 May 1919; returned, 4 Oct. 1919. Discharged (at his own request, his services being no longer required), 23 Mar. 1922.

Quest, H. O. (Monotype Staff, deputy overseer). Enlisted on 8 Jan. 1917 in the R.G.A., serving in England in the 2nd Res. H.B. to June, and thenceforward in the 2/2nd London H.B. until demobilized on 11 Jan. 1919. Resumed work at the Press.

† Rawlings, A. W. (Counting House, apprentice). Enlisted in May 1915 in the 4th Oxf. & Bucks L.I. Served in England until the following year. Posted to the 1/4th Bn. in France about Mar. 1916. Killed in action, at Pozières, on 19 July 1916.

Rawlings, A. T. (Bindery, apprentice). [Previous Service in the O.V.R.] Enlisted on 4 June 1917. Served in the Roy. Warwick Regt. To France to the 1st Bn. (Lance-Corpl.) in Feb. 1918. Transferred, in March, just after the Retirement, to the 7th D.C.L.I. Was gassed and wounded at Lens, near Arras, in May 1918, and thereafter in hospital and convalescent in England. Demobilized (from the 3rd Res. Bn. D.C.L.I.) on 30 Jan. 1919. Resumed work at the Press.

Rawlings, C. C. (Machine Room, feeder). Enlisted on 16 Feb. 1917 and posted to the 16th Worc. Regt. Was retained on Home Service throughout, serving in England and in Ireland in the 16th, 1st (Garr.), 5th, and 2nd Bns. of the Worc. Regt. Demobilized on 19 Sept. 1919.

Rawlings, E. J. (Warehouse). [Previous Service in the 4th Oxf. & Bucks L.I. for several years.] Mobilized with the 4th Oxf. & Bucks L.I. on 4 Aug. 1914, serving in England in the 1/4th Bn. until discharged, on medical grounds, on 17 Mar. 1915. Resumed work at the Press for a time. Enlisted (after several rejections) on 1 Nov. 1915 in the 156th H.B., R.G.A., and crossed to France in 1916, serving there in the R.G.A. thenceforward. Demobilized on 7 Apr. 1919.

Redhead, H. (Monotype Staff, keyboard). Enlisted on 3 Sept. 1916. Served in England in the 2/5th Bedford Regt. until discharged, on medical grounds, on 21 Feb. 1917. Resumed work at the Press.

Reid, E. C. (Bindery). Enlisted in May 1915 in the 3/4th Oxf. & Bucks L.I., remaining on Home Service in the same unit throughout. Discharged at the end of 1916, having passed the age-limit. Resumed work at the Press.

Remington, C. G. (L.S. Composing Room). Enlisted on 1 Mar. 1917 in the 196th Labour Coy. Served in the 172nd

Labour Coy. in England to 13 Mar., in France to 7 June, in Belgium to 24 Sept.; and subsequently in Italy in the 196th Labour Coy. (attd. No. 4 Sanitary Section) from 12 Oct. 1917. Demobilized on 13 Sept. 1919. Resumed work at the Press.

RENNIE, W. (Monotype Staff, compositor). [Previous Service in the 2nd V.B. Oxf. L.I.; also in the 2nd Suffolk Regt.] Enlisted on 2 Oct. 1914 in the 1st Sup. Coy., 4th Oxf. & Bucks L.I., serving in England in that unit to 29 Apr. 1916; in the R.D.C. to 2 Oct. 1916; and in the 4th Res. Bn. Oxf. & Bucks L.I. to Easter 1917. In Belgium in the 2nd Wilts Regt. until wounded and gassed at Ypres in Aug. 1917. Discharged, on account of impaired health, on 14 Feb. 1918. Resumed work at the Press.

RIVERS, S. J. (Monotype Staff, Casting Room). [Previous Service in the Territorials from Apr. 1912.] Mobilized with the 4th Oxf. & Bucks L.I. on 4 Aug. 1914, serving in the 1/4th Bn. to 8 Nov. 1914, and in the 2/4th Bn. from that date to 22 May 1916. In France in the 184th Infantry Brigade Band from 22 May 1916 to 13 Feb. 1919. Demobilized on 13 Mar. 1919.

ROBINSON, F. H. (Warehouse). Enlisted on 23 Oct. 1916 in the 4/1st Cambs Regt., serving in England throughout. In the 4/1st Cambs Transport to July 1917; attd. R.F.A. Remount Dépôt, July–Nov. 1917; then transferred to the 51st Queen's Roy. West Surrey Regt. (Brigade Clipper). Demobilized on 21 Jan. 1919. Resumed work at the Press.

ROBINSON, H. C. (Examination Paper Room). Enlisted on 14 Oct. 1916 in the R.F.A., serving in England to 28 Nov. 1917, and in France in the T.M.B., R.F.A., from that date to 14 Feb. 1918. Engagements: Épehy, Dec. 1917. Contracted septic poisoning, resulting in deformity of foot. Discharged, on account of disablement, 17 Dec. 1918. Returned to the Press (Monotype Staff, Reading Room).

ROGERS, W. J. (Machine Room, Miehle). [Previous Service in the 4th Oxf. & Bucks L.I. for two and a half years.] Enlisted on 7 Sept. 1914 in the 4th Oxf. & Bucks L.I. and served in England successively in the 1/4th Bn. and the 2/4th Bn. to 17 Mar. 1915, when he was discharged on medical grounds. Re-enlisted on 22 Nov. 1915 in the A.S.C., and served in France in that corps from 11 Dec. 1915 to 13 June 1918. Promoted Corpl. Discharged, on medical grounds, 19 Oct. 1918.

ROPER, W. L. (Machine Room, Miehle). [Previous Service in the 2nd Vol. Bn. Oxf. L.I. for five years.] On Home Service in R.A.M.C. from enlistment on 29 Mar. 1915 to demobilization on 28 May 1920. Promoted Sergt. Resumed work at the Press.

ROSE, G. W. (Bindery). Enlisted on 31 May 1915 in the 4th Oxf. & Bucks L.I., serving in England in the 3/4th Bn. to 14 Sept. 1916, and afterwards on the Army Gymnastic Staff to demobilization (attd. Roy. Horse Artillery, 19 Sept. 1916 to 5 Feb. 1919). Promoted Staff Sergt. Instructor. Demobilized on 21 Feb. 1919. Resumed work at the Press.

RUSSEN, G. F. (Machine Room, feeder, Wharfedale). Enlisted on 28 Feb. 1916 in the 28th Roy. Fusiliers, remaining on Home Service at first in that unit, later in the 13th Roy. Warwick Regt., and from Feb. 1919 in the R.A.S.C., M.T.

RYLATT, F. (Machine Room, Wharfedale). [Previous Service in the 8th Manchester Regt. for four years.] Enlisted on 4 May 1915 in the Q.O.O.H., serving in England to 20 Jan. 1918, and afterwards in Ireland (in Q.O.O.H. to Jan. 1919, and in the King's Own Roy. Liverpool Regt. to 5 May 1919). Appointed Lance-Corpl., 8 Jan. 1916; promoted Corpl., 12 Apr. 1916; Sergt., 8 Jan. 1917. Demobilized on 5 June 1919.

SAXTON, A. C. V. (Jobbing Room, hand-press, apprentice). Enlisted on 18 June 1918. Served in England in the 53rd Bn. (Y.S.) Devon Regt. until 9 July, and afterwards in the 52nd Bn. In Germany in the Army of the Rhine from 11 Mar. 1919 to 1 Mar. 1920. In hospital in Germany. Appointed Lance-Corpl., 10 Sept. 1918. Demobilized in April 1920. Resumed work at the Press.

SAXTON, H. W. (Stereo and Electro Room, apprentice). [Previous Service in the Territorials from 25 Nov. 1911.] Mobilized with the 4th Oxf. & Bucks L.I. on 4 Aug. 1914, serving in the 1/4th Bn. in England to 29 Mar. 1915 and then in France until 1 Dec. In England (invalided), in the 3/4th Res. Bn., until the following spring. Returned to France (1/4th Bn.) on 2 Apr. 1916, serving there to 28 Nov. 1917, and thenceforward in Italy. Engagements: Second Battle of Ypres, 1915; Somme, 1916; Ronssoy, 1917; Ypres, 1917; and (Italy) Asiago Plateau, 1918. Demobilized on 13 Feb. 1919. Resumed work at the Press.

† Schofield, E. (B.S. Composing Room). Enlisted on 4 June 1915 in the 4th Oxf. & Bucks L.I., training in England in the 3rd Res. Bn. Drafted to France to the 1/4th Bn. on 22 May 1916. Died on service, at Rouen, from gastro-enteritis, on 20 Dec. 1916.

† Shrimpton, R. T. (L.S. Composing Room). [Previous Service in the Q.O.O.H. from Mar. 1909.] Mobilized with the Q.O.O.H. (Sergt.) on 9 Aug. 1914, serving in England to 20 Sept. and in France from that date until 26 July 1915, when he was invalided home (appendicitis) and was in hospital to 4 Oct. Served in Ireland from 14 Oct. 1915 to Nov. 1916, and thenceforward again in France. Engagements: 1914–15—First Battle of Ypres, Loos, Arras; 1917—Guillemont Farm (raid), 21 June; Bourlon Wood, 28 Nov.; 1918—British Retirement, 21 Mar. (promoted Squadron Sergt.-Major, Apr.); British Offensive, Aug. Killed in action on 9 Aug. 1918.

Shuter, G. S. (L.S. Composing Room, apprentice). [Previous Service in the Territorials from Nov. 1913.] Mobilized with the 4th Oxf. & Bucks L.I. on 4 Aug. 1914. Posted to the 2/4th Bn. on its formation and proceeded with that unit to France on 24 May 1916. Taken prisoner at St. Quentin on 21 Mar. 1918. Repatriated on 25 Nov. 1918. Engagements: 1916—Fromelles, 19 July; Somme, Nov.: 1917—German retreat from the Somme, 25 Mar.; Passchendaele Ridge, Aug.; Cambrai, Dec.: 1918—St. Quentin (the Retirement), 21 Mar. Demobilized on 12 Mar. 1919. Resumed work at the Press.

† Simmonds, A. (Machine Room, feeder, Miehle). Enlisted in the R.A.M.C. on 25 Sept. 1915, serving in England to 3 Nov. following, and thenceforward in France. Engagements: Somme Battle, from 1 July onward. Killed in action on 13 Aug. 1916.

Simmons, A. W. (Warehouse). [Previous Service in the Press Volunteer Platoon for six months.] Enlisted on 30 Aug. 1916, and served in England in the Cambs Regt. to Mar. 1917. In France in the Queen's Roy. West Surrey Regt. from Mar. 1917 to Feb. 1918. Appointed Lance-Corpl. Health failing, he served in England (attd. A.S.C.) from Feb. to Sept. Engagement: Ypres, 31 July 1917. Discharged, on account of tachycardia, on 3 Sept. 1918. Resumed work at the Press.

Simmons, C. W. F. (Warehouse). Enlisted on 17 May 1915 in the 132nd H.B., R.G.A., serving in England to Mar. 1916, and then in France. Later attached to Heavy Brigade H.Q., and afterwards to the R.F.A., 3rd Div. Engagements: Ypres (1916), the Retirement (Mar. 1918); also other actions, including the Somme, Arras, Bapaume, Lille, Bethune, Armentières. Invalided (from Bethune) on 25 June 1918, and discharged, on account of broken health, on 26 Nov. 1918.

† SIMMS, J. (L.S. Composing Room, hand-press). Enlisted on 11 Oct. 1916, serving in England in the 1st Garr. Bn. Worcs. Regt. to Mar. 1917. Transferred to the 1st Garr. Bn. Devon Regt., and embarked for Egypt, Mar. 1917. Drowned (vessel sunk by enemy submarine) in the Mediterranean on 15 Apr. 1917.

SIMMS, P. C. (L.S. Composing Room). Enlisted on 27 July 1918, serving in England in the R.A.F. from that date to demobilization, 12 Feb. 1919. Resumed work at the Press.

SIMMS, W. G. (Machine Room, feeder, Huber). Enlisted on 18 Oct. 1915 in the 2/4th Oxf. & Bucks L.I. Was in France in that battalion until wounded at Ypres in 1917. Transferred to the 6th Oxf. & Bucks L.I., and again wounded at Ypres. After a period in hospital and convalescent in England (3rd Res. Bn.), was transferred again to the 2/4th Bn. in France. Demobilized on 5 Mar. 1919. Resumed work at the Press.

SIMS, A. (Photographic Room). Enlisted on 10 Feb. 1915, serving in England in the 2/4th Oxf. & Bucks L.I., the 52nd Oxf. & Bucks L.I., and the 13th Devon Regt. Demobilized on 27 Feb. 1919. Resumed work at the Press.

SLATTER, H. (Machine Room, feeder, Miehle). [Previous Service in the 4th Oxf. & Bucks L.I. (T.F.) for four years.] Mobilized with the 4th Oxf. & Bucks L.I. on 4 Aug. 1914, serving in the 1/4th Bn. in England to 29 Mar. 1915 and in France from that date until discharged, time-expired, 22 May 1916. Resumed work at the Press for a few weeks. Re-enlisted in the R.G.A. and served in England from 5 Aug. 1916 to 17 May 1917, and thenceforward in France. Engagements: Messines; Third Battle of Ypres; Cambrai, 1917; the Retirement (March) and the Advance, 1918. Promoted Bdr. Demobilized 10 Mar. 1919. Resumed work at the Press.

SMITH, H. D. (Delegates' Warehouse). Enlisted on 4 Nov. 1915 in the 4th Oxf. & Bucks L.I., serving in England successively in that unit, in the 83rd Prov. Bn., and in the 10th Oxf. & Bucks L.I. to 9 Jan. 1918; and from that date in Ireland in the Roy. Wilts Yeom. Demobilized on 18 Jan. 1919. Resumed work at the Press.

Smith, T. G. (Warehouse). [Previous Service in the Military Home Hospital Reserve, eight years.] Enlisted in the R.A.M.C. on 6 Aug. 1914, serving in England to Dec. 1915, and in Egypt from 15 Dec. 1915 to 20 Dec. 1918. Promoted Corpl., 1914; Sergt., 1915. Demobilized in Feb. 1919. Resumed work at the Press.

Spiers, T. F. (Bindery). [Previous Service as a Volunteer, Oxf. & Bucks L.I. (Bugle Band), for three years.] Enlisted in Aug. 1917 in the Signalling School, R.G.A. On Home Service in various batteries until sent to France in Aug. 1918 in the 114th S.B., R.G.A. (Signaller). Was in engagements on the Hindenburg Line in the Great Offensive. In hospital, through failing health, and invalided home on 6 Dec. 1918, and afterwards in hospital and convalescent until demobilization on 4 Feb. 1919. Resumed work at the Press.

Stokes, F. W. (Photographic Room). Entered the Royal Navy on 16 Feb. 1915, serving as Boy 2nd and 1st class, and Ordinary Seaman until discharge. He served afloat on H.M.S. *Warspite* from May 1915 to May 1916, and was injured in the Battle of Jutland. Discharged to shore, invalided, 5 July 1916.

Stone, E. (Bindery, apprentice). Enlisted in the R.A.M.C. on 23 Nov. 1915, serving in England to 26 Aug. 1916. In Malta (St. Andrew's Hospital) from 3 Sept. 1916 to July 1918; and in Italy (38th Stationary Hospital) from that time to 19 Mar. 1919. Demobilized on 20 May 1919. Resumed work at the Press.

Stone, P. (L.S. Composing Room, apprentice). Enlisted on 16 Feb. 1917, serving in England in the Worc. Regt. throughout. Promoted Corpl. Discharged, on medical grounds on 8 July 1919. Resumed work at the Press.

Surman, J. L. (Jobbing Room, hand-press). [Previous Service in the 2nd Vol. Bn. Oxf. L.I. for over thirty-two years; afterwards in the National Reserve.] Served as Recruiting Col.-Sergt. in Oxford for the Territorial Association from Aug. 1914 to Aug. 1915, and from that time to May 1916 for the 1st (43rd) Oxf. & Bucks L.I. recruiting area. Discharged from the Recruiting Staff on the introduction of the Derby Scheme (May 1916), and returned to work at the Press. Served as Sergt.-Major in the Oxfordshire Volunteer R.A.S.C., M.T., from 1918 until the Corps was disbanded (1921).

Surman, J. L. S. (Monotype Staff, compositor). [Previous Service in the 2nd Vol. Bn. Oxf. L.I. for four years.] Enlisted in the A.S.C. on 8 Oct. 1915, serving in England for a few days, and then in France in that Corps from 26 Oct. 1915 to Oct. 1917, and in the Labour Corps from Oct. 1917 to 20 Feb. 1919. Demobilized on 23 Mar. 1919. Resumed work at the Press.

SURMAN, J. W. (Bindery). Enlisted in the Royal Navy in Dec. 1915, serving at the R.N. Barracks, Devonport, to June 1916. With the Grand Fleet, on H.M.S. *Colossus*, from June 1916 to Dec. 1917, and on escort duty (Africa and South America) on H.M.S. *Hildebrand* from Jan. to Nov. 1918. Now A.B., R.N.

SURMAN, R. L. (Machine Room, Huber). [Previous Service in the 2nd Vol. Bn. Oxf. L.I. from 1893 (Sergt.) until the formation of the Territorials (1908), and thenceforward in the National Reserve.] Enlisted in the 1/4th Oxf. & Bucks L.I. in Sept. 1914, serving in that Bn. until Dec., and then in 2/4th Bn. Promoted Corpl.; Sergt., Feb. 1915; Warrant Officer, Class II, Mar. 1916; and transferred to R.D.C. (as Warrant Officer, Class II). Transferred in Jan. 1917 to the 16th York and Lancaster Regt., but rejected for Foreign Service on account of accidental injury sustained two years earlier. Demobilized on 31 Jan. 1919. Resumed work at the Press.

† SURMAN, T. J. (Warehouse). [Previous Service in the 2nd Vol. Bn. Oxf. L.I. (Signaller) for three years; afterwards in the National Reserve for several years.] Enlisted on 19 Sept. 1914 in the 4th Oxf. & Bucks L.I., serving in the 2/4th Bn. (Sergt.) in England to 24 May 1916, and in France from that time to the July following. Engagements: Auber's Ridge; Laventie, 19 July 1916. Wounded in the latter engagement and died of wounds on 14 Aug. 1916.

TAUNTON, A. W. (Monotype Staff, keyboard). Enlisted in the Q.O.O.H. on 24 Oct. 1916, serving in the 2/1st Q.O.O.H. in England to 19 Jan. 1918, and in Ireland to 11 Jan. 1919. Promoted Corpl. Demobilized on 12 Jan. 1919. Resumed work at the Press.

TAYLOR, C. H. (Secretary's Office). Enlisted on 7 Sept. 1914 in the 4th Oxf. & Bucks L.I., serving in the 1/4th Bn. in England to 29 Mar. 1915 and then in France to Apr. 1917. Wounded (gunshot) at Guillemont Farm. In hospital in England to July and with the 3/4th Bn. to Nov. In the 4th Nigeria Regt. in East Africa from Nov. 1917 to Feb. 1918, and in Nigeria from that time to Mar. 1919. Engagements: Somme, July and Aug. 1916; (Nigeria) Abeokuta Rebellion. Promoted Sergt., 1917. Demobilized on 5 June 1919. Resumed work at the Press.

Taylor, E. H. (Engineers' workshop). Enlisted on 25 July 1916 and served, in England throughout, in the Durham L.I. to June 1918; in the 33rd Lond. Regt. to Aug. 1918; in the Hotchkiss Gun Coy. (attd. 226th Brigade) to Dec. 1918; and in the R.D.C. to demobilization on 23 Jan. 1919. Resumed work at the Press.

Taylor, E. H. J. (Monotype Staff, compositor). Enlisted in Nov. 1915 in the 156th R.G.A. Accidentally injured (gassed) in the period of training, and retained on Home Service in consequence. Appointed Lance-Bdr. Employed on anti-aircraft work from 1917 in the 14th A.A. Coy. (Bdr.). Demobilized on 27 Jan. 1919. Resumed work at the Press.

Taylor, G. S. (Stereo and Electro Room). [Previous Service in the 2nd (V.B.) Oxf. & Bucks L.I. for four years.] Enlisted in Apr. 1917, serving in England in the 3rd Res. Bn. Oxf. & Bucks L.I. to June, and then in France in the 1st Bucks Bn. (T.F.) until wounded (gunshot, in head and shoulder) on 16 Aug. In England in the 3rd Res. Bn., in hospital &c. to Dec. 1917. Transferred to the R.A.S.C. (M.T.) and served in England to Mar. 1918 and in Italy from that time onward. Engagement: Paschendaele Ridge. Demobilized in Feb. 1919. Resumed work at the Press.

Taylor, G. W. (Warehouse). Enlisted in July 1918, serving in the R.A.S.C., H.T. (Driver), in England to demobilization in Mar. 1919. Resumed work at the Press.

Taylor, P. H. (L.S. Composing Room). Enlisted in Sept. 1914 in the 4th Oxf. & Bucks L.I., serving in England to the following June. In France in the 1/4th Bn. from June 1915 to Dec. 1916. Slightly wounded at that date, and subsequently on Home Service in the 3/4th Bn. from Jan. 1917 to demobilization. Engagements: Somme; trench warfare, July to Dec. 1916. Appointed Lance-Sergt. Demobilized on 27 Jan. 1919. Resumed work at the Press.

Thomas, A. H. (Strong Room). Enlisted in Sept. 1914. Served for a time in the 7th Oxf. & Bucks L.I., and later in the Army Pay Corps.

Thomas, H. C. (L.S. Composing Room). Enlisted on 8 June 1918 in the R.A.M.C., and, after a period of training in the North of England, served in France, from September, in a Sanitary Squad. Demobilized on 17 Feb. 1919. Resumed work at the Press.

Timbs, W. R. (Bindery). Enlisted on 25 Sept. 1916, and served in England in the 2/5th Bedford Regt. to Mar. 1917.

In the 139th Labour Coy. in France from 25 Mar. to Oct. 1917, and in Belgium from that date to 1 Jan. 1919; and again in France, in the 50th Labour Coy. to 12 Feb. Served in France at Arras, Souchy, Vimy, and in Belgium in the Ypres sector; was in the Final Advance, Oct.–Nov. 1918. Demobilized on 19 Feb. 1919.

Timms, J. A. (Machine Room, feeder, Huber). [Previous Service in the Army, 2nd Roy. Berks Regt.] Called up as reservist, on the outbreak of war, with the 2nd Roy. Berks Regt., and served in France in that unit from Aug. 1914 for two years. Wounded in shoulder, after the Battle of Loos, Aug. 1916. Discharged, on account of wound, 25 Aug. 1916. Resumed work at the Press.

Tomkins, A. (Warehouse). Enlisted on 31 Aug. 1915 in the Oxf. & Bucks L.I., serving in England in the 3rd (Res.) Bn. to 14 Feb. 1916. Posted to the 1st Bn. and served in Mesopotamia from 11 Mar. to 5 Aug. 1916, and in India from 21 Aug. 1916 to 28 Jan. 1919. Engagements: with General Aylmer's Kut Relief Force; San-y-Yat, 22 Apr. 1916. Appointed Lance-Corpl. Several times in hospital—malarial fever, heat-stroke, &c. Demobilized on 4 Apr. 1919. Resumed work at the Press.

Tomkins, P. G. (Machine Room, counter). Enlisted on 11 Nov. 1915, serving in the 14th Worcs. Regt. in England to 20 June 1916, and in France and Belgium for two years from that date, until wounded (in thigh) by bomb from enemy aeroplane on 16 June 1918. Thenceforward in England. In hospital from June to Sept.; in the 6th Worc. Regt., Sept. to Dec.; and in the Labour Corps from Dec. to demobilization. Engagements: Ancre, Nov. 1916; Somme, Dec. 1916 to Mar. 1917; Arras, Apr. to Sept.; Passchendaele, Sept. to Dec.; Cambrai (and the Retirement), Dec. 1917 to 21 Mar. 1918. Demobilized on 14 Jan. 1919. Resumed work at the Press.

Tomlinson, W. (Monotype Staff, compositor). Enlisted on 18 July 1916, serving in England in the 2/1st Durham L.I. to 14 Mar. 1918, and in the 29th City of London Regt. thenceforward to demobilization on 26 Jan. 1919. Resumed work at the Press.

Tooby, A. E. (L.S. Composing Room). Enlisted on 29 Nov. 1915; served in England throughout, in the 18th Hants Regt. and various other units. Member of Portsmouth Garrison Fire Brigade; Motor Tractor Driver and Ploughman. Demobilized on 2 Feb. 1919. Resumed work at the Press.

Traill, W. E. (L.S. Composing Room). Enlisted in June 1918 and was retained on Home Service. Served in the 116th Coy. I.W.D., R.E., at Sandwich (three months), at Poole, and at Slough. Demobilized on 23 Dec. 1918. Resumed work at the Press.

Tratt, E. (L.S. Composing Room). Enlisted on 1 Nov. 1915 in the 4th Oxf. & Bucks L.I. and was retained on Home Service throughout, serving successively in the 3/4th Oxf. & Bucks L.I., the 83rd Prov. Bn., and the 13th Devons (Works Bn.). Discharged on medical grounds in June 1917. Resumed work at the Press.

Tuffrey, A. H. M. (L.S. Warehouse). [Previous Service in the 4th Oxf. & Bucks L.I. for two years.] Mobilized with the 4th Oxf. & Bucks L.I. on 4 Aug. 1914, serving in England in the 1/4th Bn. and crossing to France in that unit on 29 Mar. 1915. Appointed Lance-Corpl. Invalided in Aug. 1916 and transferred to the 3/4th Bn. Returned to France in May 1917 (Corpl.) in the 2/1st Bucks Bn. (shortly afterwards merged in the 2/4th Bn.). Engagements: Somme, 1 July 1916; Cambrai, Nov. 1917; the Retirement, Mar. 1918. Wounded (gunshot, both thighs) in Mar. 1918 and returned to England in April. Demobilized on 9 Jan. 1919. Resumed work at the Press.

Turner, N. W. (Monotype Staff, Casting Room). Enlisted on 3 May 1915 in the Oxf. & Bucks L.I. Served in the 4th Res. Bn. in England until posted to the 1/4th Bn. in France in Jan. 1916. Wounded in the Advance of July 1916, gunshot wound in knee and shrapnel wound in shoulder. In England (hospital, &c.) for six months. Again in France, in the 2/4th Bn., from Feb. 1917. Gassed in the following Oct. In England (hospital &c.) to Feb. 1918. Transferred to the 11th Queen's Roy. West Surrey Regt. and returned to France, serving there and in Germany until demobilization. Appointed Lance-Corpl. Engagements: Somme, 1–23 July 1916; Ypres, Aug. 1917. Demobilized on 21 Mar. 1919.

Turner, S. J. (Secretary's Office). Enlisted in the 4th Oxf. & Bucks L.I. on 3 Sept. 1914, serving in the 1/4th Bn. in England and crossing to France in that unit on 29 Mar. 1915. Left the battalion a few days later and served at 48th Div. H.Q. as draughtsman until Mar. 1916; at the Fourth Army H.Q., in charge of the General Staff draughtsmen's office. Transferred to the R.E. early in 1917, was subsequently promoted Sergt., remaining with the Fourth Army until demobilized on 15 Apr. 1919.

Van den Oever, P. (Photographic Room). Served in the Belgian forces, in France and Belgium. In the Infantry C.I. 4 from enlistment (as Pte., 5 Oct. 1916) to 8 Jan. 1917; in the 2nd Regt. H. Battery to 6 Mar. 1917; and thenceforward in the 1st Regt. H. Battery. Engagements: Somme, Mar. 1917; La Folie, Le Roye, St. Quentin (with the French Army); and Dixmude (Belgium), Oct.–Nov. 1917. Demobilized on 25 July 1919.

Waine, S. (L.S. Composing Room, apprentice). [Previous Service in the Q.O.O.H. for three years.] Mobilized with the Q.O.O.H. (Corpl.) on 4 Aug. 1914, serving in England to 20 Sept. 1914; in France from that date to 10 Oct. 1916; and again in England from 26 Oct. 1916 to 27 Nov. 1917. Thenceforward in France in the M.G.C. (2nd Lt.). Engagements: All Q.O.O.H. engagements up to Oct. 1916; the Retirement (from St. Quentin), Mar. 1918; and the Final Advance Oct.–Nov. 1918, finishing in line at Maubeuge. Appointed Lance-Sergt. 22 Nov. and promoted Sergt. 24 Dec. 1914. Gazetted 2nd Lt., 25 Sept. 1917; Lt., 26 Mar. 1919. Military Medal (gazetted 10 Nov. 1916). Demobilized on 19 May 1919.

† Wakelin, H. W. (Warehouse, White Paper Room). [Previous Service in the R.A.M.C. from 2 Nov. 1896; South African War (Queen's Medal, clasp, King's Medal, clasp).] Enlisted in the R.A.M.C. on 12 Sept. 1914, serving in England until early in 1918, and then in Salonika to 1919. Promoted Corpl., 9 Jan. 1915; Sergt. 15 May 1915. Was serving at Constantinople in the spring of 1919, and was on the point of returning to England for demobilization, when he received a cut whilst engaged on post-mortem work, and died from blood-poisoning on 15 Apr. 1919.

Walker, A. (Machine Room, feeder, Miehle). Enlisted on 4 May 1917, serving in England in the Duke of Cornwall's L.I. and in the Roy. Warwick Regt. to March 1918, and thenceforward in France in the Duke of Cornwall's L.I. Engagements: St. Quentin (the Retirement), Mar.; Douai (the Final Advance), 5 Oct. Wounded once, in leg, arm, and face. Demobilized in 1919.

Walker, A. V. J. (Secretary's Office). Enlisted on 3 Oct. 1916, serving in England in the 100th (S.) Coy., Army Ordnance Corps, to 1 Apr. 1917, and from that date onward in No. 3 S.D., Royal Flying Corps and Royal Air Force. Promoted Corpl. (R.A.F.). Demobilized on 3 Apr. 1919. Resumed work at the Press.

Walker, G. D. N. (Photographic Room). Enlisted in the 4th Oxf. & Bucks L.I. on 5 Sept. 1914, serving in the 1/4th Bn. in England to 29 Mar. 1915; in France from that date to 8 Dec. 1916; in England (hospital and convalescent, frost-bitten feet) for the following twelve months. Returned to France in the 2/4th Bn., serving there from 8 Dec. 1917 until wounded (left foot, shrapnel) on 2 Nov. 1918; and thenceforward in England (hospital and convalescent). Engagements: Somme, Cambrai, St. Quentin. Discharged, on account of wound, 22 Jan. 1919. Resumed work at the Press.

Walker, W. (Jobbing Room, messenger). Enlisted on 15 June 1918, serving in England in the R.A.M.C. to October, and then in Ireland until demobilized in Jan. 1919. Resumed work at the Press.

Walker, W. T. (L.S. Reading Room). [Previous Service in the 2nd Vol. Bn. Oxf. L.I., 1892–5.] Enlisted in the 1st Sup. Coy. 4th Oxf. & Bucks L.I. on 2 Oct. 1914, serving in England in that Coy. to 29 Apr. 1916; and thenceforward in the 258th Protection Coy., R.D.C. Appointed Lance-Corpl. Demobilized on 26 Jan. 1919. Resumed work at the Press.

Wallen, L. C. F. (Machine Room, feeder, Wharfedale). Enlisted in the Royal Navy (Seaman) on 15 Jan. 1915, serving on H.M.S. *Powerful* to 15 Apr., H.M.S. *Essex* (Atlantic Ocean) to 7 Aug. 1916, H.M.S. *Pembroke* to 4 Oct. 1916, H.M.S. *Africa* (Mediterranean and West African waters) to 12 May 1918, H.M.S. *Actaeon* to 6 Dec. 1918. Continuing service.

† Wallen, W. H. G. (Machine Room, feeder, Miehle). Enlisted on 4 Nov. 1915, serving in England in the Q.O.O.H. to 15 Dec. 1916, and in France in the 2/4th Oxf. & Bucks L.I. from 18 Dec. onward. Wounded at La Maisonette and died of wounds two days later, 28 Feb. 1917.

Ward, W. J. (Machine Room, Wharfedale, apprentice). Enlisted on 10 May 1916, serving in the 3/1st Q.O.O.H. in England to 7 June and then in Ireland to 9 Dec. In France, in the 1/4th Oxf. & Bucks L.I., from 10 Dec. 1916 to 25 Mar. 1917. Contracted septic poisoning whilst on active service and was in England (hospital and convalescent) to 25 Aug. and in Ireland to 12 Nov.; then in the 3/4th (Res.) Bn. to 21 Jan. 1918. Transferred to the 7th Bn. and served in the

Balkans to Apr. 1919, and subsequently in Egypt (Army of Occupation). Engagements: La Maisonette and Peronne, Feb. and Mar. 1917; Bulgarian Retreat, 21 Sept. to 2 Oct. 1918. Demobilized on 5 Dec. 1919. Resumed work at the Press.

Warmington, C. (Bindery Office). Enlisted on 26 Aug. 1918, serving in the 53rd Roy. Warwick Regt. in England to 17 Mar. 1919, and in Germany with the British Army of the Rhine from that time to 26 Oct. (attd. to Motor Transport service for three weeks, June–July), and thenceforward in the 51st Bn. Left Germany 6 Feb.; demobilized 12 Feb. 1920.

Watts, R. H. (Photographic Room). Enlisted on 16 Aug. 1915 in the Oxf. & Bucks L.I., serving in England in the 3/4th Bn. to Apr. 1918. Served in France, Belgium, and Germany in the 2nd Bn. Oxf. & Bucks L.I. from 4 Apr. to 22 Dec. 1918. Engagements: Gommecourt, 22 Aug.; Sapigny, 25 Aug.; Rumilly, 1 Oct. Promoted Sergt.; Signalling Instructor. Wounded (severely) by gas shell; suffered from trench fever and from influenza. Demobilized on 12 Apr. 1919.

Webb, G. W. (Monotype Staff, compositor). [Previous Service in the Territorials for over seven years.] Mobilized with the 4th Oxf. & Bucks L.I. (Bugler) on 4 Aug. 1914, serving in England in the 1/4 Bn. to 29 Mar. 1915, and in France and Belgium to 29 May 1915. Wounded (in trench warfare) in left forearm; scalp wounds; loss of right eye. Served in England in the 83rd Prov. Bn. until discharged, on account of wounds, on 14 Mar. 1916. Resumed work at the Press.

Webb, H. (Stereo and Electro Room). [Previous Service in the Roy. Berks Regt., for fourteen months.] Enlisted in the Roy. Berks Regt. on 28 Dec. 1914, serving in England to the following August. In France, in the M.G.C., from 7 Aug. 1915 to 21 Nov. 1918. Discharged, on account of influenza, on 13 Feb. 1919.

Weller, H. T. (Monotype Staff, compositor, apprentice). Enlisted in the 4th Oxf. and Bucks L.I. on 15 Sept. 1914, serving in the 2/4th Bn. in England to May 1916, and in France from 24 May 1916 to 17 May 1917. Wounded (gun-shot) in right shoulder, neck, and foot. Thenceforward on Home Service—hospital and convalescent to October, and subsequently in the 2/1st Roy. Devon Yeom. to Jan. 1919. Engagements: Somme, end of 1916; St. Quentin, early 1917. Promoted Corpl. Demobilized on 22 Jan. 1919. Resumed work at the Press.

West, L. G. (Secretary's Office). Enlisted in the 4th Oxf. & Bucks L.I. on 3 Sept. 1914, serving in the 1/4th Bn. in England to 29 Mar. 1915. Reached France in that Bn. on 30 Mar. 1915. At a later date was transferred to the R.E. (Sapper), remaining in France to 10 Jan. 1919. Meritorious Service Medal. Demobilized in Jan. 1919. Resumed work at the Press.

Whareham, H. W. (Bindery). [Previous Service in the Territorials for four years; National Reserve.] Enlisted on 7 Sept. 1914 in the 4th Oxf. & Bucks L.I. Retained on Home Service throughout. Served in the 1/4th Bn. to Nov.; in the 2/4th Bn. to Aug. 1915; in the 83rd Prov. Bn. to Nov. 1916; in the 10th Bn. to July 1917; and then in the 2/1st Roy. Wilts Yeom., in England to Jan. 1918 and afterwards in Ireland. Appointed Lance-Corpl., Feb. 1915; promoted Corpl., July 1915; Sergt., June 1917; Instructor in Musketry, Anti-Gas, and Infantry Training. Demobilized on 25 Feb. 1919. Resumed work at the Press.

Whitaker, R. A. (Photographic Room). Enlisted on 10 Apr. 1917 in the 7th Worc. Regt., serving in that unit in England for a few weeks (to 22 June), and in India from 27 Sept. 1917. Transferred on 10 Oct. 1918 to the 282nd Coy., M.G.C., and continued service in India to 15 Dec. 1919. Promoted Sergt. (appointed A/Paymaster). Demobilized on 10 Jan. 1920. Resumed work at the Press.

† White, B. H. (Machine Room, Wharfedale). Enlisted on 14 Aug. 1916, serving in England in the A.O.C. to 12 Apr. 1917, and afterwards in the 1/7th Worc. Regt., in which unit he went to France on 12 July. Engagements: Passchendaele Ridge, 26 Sept. and 9–10 Oct. Killed in action on 10 Oct. 1917.

Whiting, A. E. (Monotype Staff, Casting Room). Enlisted on 21 Jan. 1915 in the Royal Marine L.I. He was engaged in the landing at the Dardanelles, and at a later date was sent ashore in France with guns and was taken prisoner by the Germans in the Battle of the Somme, on 28 Apr. 1917. Repatriated 29 Dec. 1918. Now in the Royal Navy.

Whiting, S. H. (Monotype Staff, Casting Room). Enlisted on 8 Feb. 1917, serving in England in the R.F.C. to 16 Jan. 1920, and then in Germany (Inter-Allied Commission of Control, Aeronautical) in the R.A.F. Demobilized on 24 July 1920. Resumed work at the Press.

WICKENS, H. C. W. (Machine Room, feeder, Wharfedale and Platen). Enlisted in the 4th Oxf. & Bucks L.I. on 9 Sept. 1915, and served in England in the 3/4th Bn. until May 1916. Entered the Royal Navy on 9 Sept. 1916. Served in Home waters on board H.M.S. *Queen Elizabeth* to Oct. 1919 (A.B.). Was present at the Surrender of the German Fleet. [Has since seen service, on H.M.S. *Versatile*, in Russian waters (bombardment of Libau and Riga, Oct.–Dec. 1919) and in the Mediterranean.]

WICKS, G. A. (Monotype Staff, compositor). Enlisted in Oct. 1915, serving in England in the 156th H.B., R.G.A., to Sept. 1916. In France in the 16th H.B.; afterwards (in the 19th H.B.) in Belgium, and in Italy (Nov. 1917 to Feb. 1919). Engagements: Somme; Pilkem; Asiago Plateau; River Piave. Wounded (gunshot) in right shoulder. Demobilized on 2 Mar. 1919. Resumed work at the Press.

WILLETT, E. (Machine Room, Miehle). Enlisted on 29 Apr. 1915 in the Q.O.O.H. Posted to the Westmorland and Cumberland Yeomanry in France early in 1916; transferred later to the Border Regt., serving first in the 5th Bn. and afterwards in the 7th Bn. Invalided in Mar. 1918 and sent home in May. After a period of hospital and convalescence, was retained on Home Service in the 3rd Bn. Border Regt. In various engagements, including Passchendaele and the Retirement of Mar. 1918. Demobilized on 28 Feb. 1919. Resumed work at the Press.

WILLIAMS, J. H. (Counting House). [Previous Service in the Territorials from Feb. 1911.] Mobilized with the 4th Oxf. & Bucks L.I. on 4 Aug. 1914, serving in the 1/4th Bn. in England to 29 Mar. 1915, and in France from that time until invalided by shell-shock. Engaged in trench warfare, 1915. Discharged, on account of neurasthenia, on 16 Feb. 1916. Resumed work at the Press.

WILLIAMS, W. H. P. (L.S. Accent Store, apprentice). [Previous Service in the 4th Oxf. & Bucks L.I. for eighteen months.] Mobilized with the 4th Oxf. & Bucks L.I. on 4 Aug. 1914, serving in England in the 1/4th Bn., afterwards in the 2/4th Bn., and later in the Tank Corps (Driver). Served in France in the Tank Corps. Demobilized on 3 Feb. 1919. Resumed work at the Press.

WILLOUGHBY, A. F. (L.S. Reading Room). Enlisted on 20 May 1915, serving in the 2/6th Roy. Sussex Regt. in England to 4 Feb. 1916, and in India from Feb. 1916 to Dec. 1919. Engagements: NW. Frontier, Waziristan, capture of

Nanu, 1917; Afghan Campaign, 1919; Amritsar Rising, 1919. Promoted Sergt. Demobilized on 11 Dec. 1919. Resumed work at the Press.

WILLOUGHBY, W. N. (Lithographic Room, apprentice). Enlisted in the R.A.M.C. on 16 Nov. 1914, serving with the 2/3rd Wessex Field Ambulance to 13 Feb. 1917 in England, and then for six months in France. Sent home to train for commission and was in the 21st O.C.B. from 9 Aug. 1917 to 25 Mar. 1918. Gazetted 2nd Lt., Roy. Berks Regt., serving with the 4th Bn. in England to 26 Aug., and from that time with the 8th Bn. in France to 26 Oct., when he was gassed. Engagements: Armentières, July 1917; German Retreat, 1918. Demobilized on 3 Apr. 1919.

† WINSTONE, A. E. (Secretary's Office). [Previous Service in the O.V.T.C. for about six months until enlistment.] Enlisted in Aug. 1916, serving in England in the R.F.C. (2nd A/M.) to the following February, and in France from Feb. to Oct. 1917. He served at Ypres and elsewhere, but few details are known. He was killed in action in Belgium on 20 Oct. 1917.

WINSTONE, C. V. (Machine Room, Wharfedale). Enlisted on 5 Sept. 1914 in the 4th Oxf. & Bucks. L.I., serving in England in the 1/4th Bn. to Mar. 1915, in the 2/4th Bn. to Dec. 1915, and in the 83rd Prov. Bn. (with O.T.C.) until discharged, on account of bronchial disability, on 4 Aug. 1916. Resumed work at the Press.

WINTERBORNE, T. J. (Machine Room, feeder, Miehle). Enlisted on 30 Sept. 1918, serving in England in the R.A.F. until demobilized on 30 Mar. 1919.

WOODCOCK, J. G. (Machine Room, Wharfedale). Enlisted in the R.G.A. on 4 Dec. 1915, serving in England in the 43rd Coy. (to 10 June) and in the 191st H.B. (to 20 Jan. 1917), and thenceforward in France in the 1/1st Essex H.B. Engagements: Vimy Ridge, 9 Apr. 1917; Passchendaele, Nov. 1917; British Offensive near Amiens, 8 Aug. 1918; Hindenburg Line, Oct. 1918. Demobilized 2 Mar. 1919.

WOODWARD, A. G. (Photographic Room). Enlisted in the 4th Oxf. & Bucks L.I. on 16 Aug. 1915, serving in England until posted to the 1/4th Bn. in France on 12 Oct. 1917. In Italy with the 1/4th Bn. from 27 Nov. 1917 to 12 Feb. 1919. Engagement: Asiago Plateau, 15 June 1918. Appointed Lance-Corpl.; 1st Cl. Signaller. Wounded (slightly) at Asiago; fever, 1918. Demobilized on 25 Apr. 1919.

† WOODWARD, D. G. H. (Stereo and Electro Room). Enlisted in the 4th Oxf. & Bucks L.I. in May 1915, serving in England until posted to the 1/4th Bn. in France in Mar. 1916. In Italy with the 1/4th Bn. from 27 Nov. 1917 until June 1918. Wounded in shoulder and chest at Asiago Plateau, 15 June, and died of wounds a week later (22 June 1918).

WOODWARD, F. J. (Counting House). Enlisted in the R.G.A. on 8 Apr. 1916, serving in England to 31 Mar. 1917, in Belgium to November, and in France from 10 Nov. 1917 to 13 Feb. 1919. Engagements: Messines, 1917; Cambrai, Nov. 1917; Flanders, 30 July to 9 Nov. 1917; Retirement and Advance on the Somme, 1918. Promoted Bombardier. Wounded by shrapnel; shell-shock. Demobilized 14 Feb. 1919. Resumed work at the Press.

WRIGHT, J. T. (Examination Paper Room). [Previous Service in the Volunteers for three years.] Enlisted in the 4th Oxf. & Bucks L.I. on 18 Jan. 1915, serving in the 2/4th Bn. in England to 25 May 1916, and thenceforward in France until Mar. 1918. Engagements: All with the 61st Division. Taken prisoner in the Retirement of Mar. 1918, remaining in Germany to the December following. Promoted Sergt. Demobilized on 30 Mar. 1919. Resumed work at the Press.

YOUNG, A. H. R. (L.S. Reading Room). Enlisted in the R.A.M.C. on 23 Nov. 1915, serving at the Military Hospital, Preston Barracks, Brighton (A/Lance-Corpl.) to 3 Dec. 1916, and at the Dépôt, Aldershot, until embarkation on Christmas Day. *En route* to Mesopotamia until 23 Mar. 1917. At the 21st Indian General Hospital, Amara (X-ray operator), from 20 Apr. 1917 to 3 Apr. 1919. Detained in India on the way home, serving at No. 19 British General Hospital, Rawalpindi (NW. Frontier Rising; Afghan Campaign), from 20 May to 4 Sept. 1919. Demobilized on 21 Oct. 1919. Resumed work at the Press.

THE HOME-COMING

Among the many plans upset by the outbreak of war was the intended celebration in 1914 of the twenty-first anniversary of the opening of the Clarendon Press Institute. In the hope that the fighting would soon be over the event was deferred to 1915—and again deferred, year by year. It took place in September 1919, and took the form of a full week's programme of well-assorted entertainments. The chief and final event was the Dinner and Welcome Home to the returned soldiers, on Saturday, 20 September. It was a great occasion. The tables were laid for more than 250, and the large hall was decorated with flags and bright with the newly installed electric light. The chair was occupied by Mr. Charles Cannan, Secretary to the Delegates of the Press and President of the Institute, and the company present also included Mr. J. A. R. Marriott, M.P., Sir Robert Buckell (the Mayor), the Dean of Christ Church, the Principal of Brasenose, the Provost of Oriel, Mr. F. J. Hall (Controller of the Press), Captain R. W. Chapman, Mr. J. de M. Johnson, Lt.-Col. G. S. A. Ranking, C.M.G., Mr. W. C. Burnet, Mr. P. E. Matheson, Mr. D. H. Nagel, Mr. D. G. Hogarth, Mr. D. Clapperton, Councillors S. Hutchins, C. Harris, W. King, J.P., and E. C. Armstead, Mr. A. H. Frimbley, J.P., Mr. Brownrigg, and Mr. John Mansell (first secretary of the Institute).

An extended report of this event can be found in *The Clarendonian* for October 1919, but it should be said here that midway through the toast list the Controller proposed ' Our Returned Members ', and that five members responded, representing service in various fields, namely Captain R. W. Chapman (Salonika), Lieut. L. R. Griffin (France), Corpl. H. R. Goddard (Italy), Pte. R. H. New (East Africa), and Lance-Corpl. F. Ludlow (Home Defence).

THE 'GARDEN QUAD'

WAR WORK AT HOME

It remains to give some account of how others, continuing to follow their employment at the Press, contributed tirelessly and in many ways to the common aim—victory. Here, at the Press, in the course of the daily work, men—and women —'did the State some service'.

WAR PRINTING

The War was yet in its early stages when those who, in London, were responsible for the perfecting of arrangements for carrying on hostilities turned their eyes to Oxford and found there what they sought—a staff fully equipped and able to produce the most intricate and special letterpress printing, no matter what the language; skilled too in the preparation and printing of maps; and unhesitatingly ready to undertake any order, however arduous or exacting. Thus the Press was put into commission, and the volume of its War work steadily grew. In 1917 and 1918 it was not unusual to have 200 employees engaged on War printing—the women and girls contributing of their best, eager to do their share equally with the men and boys.

In his speech at the unveiling of the War Memorial Sir Reginald Hall referred to this work as 'of vital importance in winning the War'. Thus the men who in the evenings were digging and planting, or attending at hospitals or at the Fire Station, or performing War duties of other kinds, were engaged during the day on work that was no whit less important. And while the Recruiting Officers were appealing at the Tribunals for these very men, not knowing the nature of the work on which they were engaged, the Admiralty and other Whitehall Departments were demanding more and more printing from them, urgency often necessitating night work. Both parties in the end were satisfied; and that the usual Oxford standard of printing was maintained is shown by the following extracts from letters received at the Press from men whose business it was to see that the work was produced with accuracy and speed:

'I am directed by . . . to convey to you the expression of his thanks and of his appreciation of the remarkably punctual and expeditious manner in which the Oxford University Press has discharged its task.'

'I am greatly indebted to the Oxford University Press for the successful accomplishment of the work.'

'I am more than satisfied with the excellent arrangements made for the rapidity of the production.'

Looking back on those years when, united by a common peril and inspired with a common purpose, all worked with unflagging zeal, it is pleasant to recall how much was accomplished. Laborious days were the rule. The close of the working day at the Press was the opportunity for 'doing a bit' in some other field of service. First place among the patriotic spare-time enterprises of that period must be given to the Press Volunteer Platoon; but the spirit of those redoubtable 'G.R.'s' marked every other enterprise, down to the minor undertakings that can scarcely now be rescued from oblivion. For example, the following appeared one day upon the notice-boards:

SEPTEMBER 28 (SATURDAY AFTERNOON) AND 29 (SUNDAY MORNING), 1918

MINISTRY OF NATIONAL SERVICE

Twenty Volunteers Wanted from Press to dig 40 poles of potatoes at Headington for Hospital. Boy Scouts will pick up. Conveyance will start from Institute 1.30 p.m. Saturday.

F. W. BARNARD will furnish particulars.

The 'Twenty Volunteers' were forthcoming. At another time the Chairman of the Land Cultivation Committee (Alderman the Provost of Oriel) called at the Press and asked for a squad of volunteers to level the land which had been thrown up to form a riding ring on Port Meadow. About a score of men devoted three evenings to this work. These purely voluntary services are but samples of many. Fees and rewards were out of the reckoning.

PRESS VOLUNTEER PLATOON

The War was still in its early days when, at the instance of Mr. A. D. Godley, a number of Oxford 'veterans' began drilling, with guardian eyes on 'the last ditch'. An active part in the formation of this corps was taken by certain Press men, chief among them being the late Mr. George Denton, whose reserves of energy were already laid under heavy contribution by his many responsibilities at the Press. Early Instructors of the squad were the late Colour-Sergt. Joseph Brown (clicker of one of the three 'ships of apprentices), Sergt. Alfred Bowen (of the Counting House), and Sergt. Walter Bowen (of the Oriental 'ship). Each of these had a long Volunteer and Territorial record, Mr. Brown's time-limit having been passed (much to his regret) some two or three years earlier.

From the strictly military viewpoint the squad at that time may have seemed a somewhat nebulous 'unit'; in the view of the average citizen it was a patriotic body, worthy to be encouraged with unlimited good-humoured chaff; looked back upon from the present time it stands out conspicuously among the patriotic enterprises of those Press men who carried on at home. To set forth adequately the abounding zeal and energy of the Press Platoon is no easy task; to over-rate them is hardly possible.

Although the ardour of these 'last-liners' was admirable from the outset, the hour of official recognition was deferred. When the Rifle Volunteer movement developed and the 1st Bn. Oxfordshire Volunteer Training Corps (the V.T.C.) was formed, the squad acquired a more definite standing and furnished the nucleus of No. 8 Platoon, B Company, under Platoon-Commander W. C. Burnet (later Lieut., R.G.A., now Secretary to the Oxford Local Examinations Delegacy). It was a stroke of rare good fortune for the Platoon to have Lieut. Burnet as its first officer. His painstaking thoroughness kept the ardour burning and the efficiency steadily rising. His enthusiasm was contagious, and before long the members found themselves subscribing towards the cost of their grey-green uniforms.

Beginning with a roll of from forty to fifty, all above the military age, the Platoon had at one time a strength of well over sixty. Its numbers, however, fluctuated considerably. Younger men came in—and passed out again, to somewhere nearer the front line. Men who had never before handled a rifle learned to shoot, and shoot well; and gradually the Platoon became a recruiting ground for the Army, sending altogether between forty and fifty men into His Majesty's Forces. Lieut. Burnet himself was one of the early ones to pass into the Army, but he left his mark on the Press Platoon; to him as much as to any one is due the success it attained. There were a few who remained members from beginning to end. Sergt. F. Bascombe (of the Entry Office) acted as secretary to the Platoon.

The 'G.R.'s' (so called from the letters on their brassards) in their strict attention to business suffered other names also with commendable imperturbability, such for instance as 'Granny's Reserves', 'Godley's Rascals', 'German Ruffians'. The name was *not* the guinea stamp: the gold was there for all that!

The Volunteer Training Corps (V.T.C.) in due course developed into the Oxfordshire Volunteer Regiment, and the Press Platoon, like the rest, took unto itself the new uniform. Later on, permission was given to change the style of the Regiment to 1st Vol. Bn. the Oxfordshire and Buckinghamshire Light Infantry, and upon the new caps appeared the honourable badge of the famous Oxford and Bucks.

B 8 continued to do well and to accumulate good marks. Hence when they had the option of taking the place of one or other of the platoons that had fallen out, they declined, preferring to remain B 8—which they did, until their disbandment. One of their greatest successes was achieved in the competition for the Penny Challenge Cup (so named after the donor, Mr. F. P. Penny), points being awarded for turn-out, for marching, and for shooting. Eight platoons competed, and B 8 were runners-up and only a few points behind the winners (A 4).

On the departure of Lieut. Burnet the platoon command was taken over by 2nd Lieut. J. S. Arthur, Science Master of the Oxford High School. When he too went into the Army (he was awarded the O.B.E. for work on water supplies) his successor was 2nd Lieut. Brownrigg. The next appointment was nearer home. Colour-Sergt. Joseph Brown having died, and Sergts. Alfred and Walter Bowen having donned the regulation khaki, Sergt. Walter Collier (of the Counting House) became Platoon Sergeant; and when Lieut. Brownrigg was promoted to the command of a Company, Sergt. Collier was gazetted 2nd Lieut. and given charge of the Platoon.

Drills and exercises were carried out with keenness. Lieut. Collier, Sergt. F. Bryan (of the Counting House), and Corpl. H. E. Mapleston (of the Reading Department) attended a School of Musketry and gained Instructors' Certificates. Also, Lieut. Collier underwent a week's training at Candahar Barracks, Tidworth, and Corpl. Mapleston attended two courses at a Bombing School and (in quite another field of study) gained the St. John Ambulance certificate for First Aid.

The Platoon supplied guards at various places (the railway lines, the Riding School, Leafield Wireless Station, &c.), and some strenuous work was done on several occasions at Banbury Stores and regularly on Saturday afternoons and Sundays at Didcot Ordnance Dépôt.[1] Of these duties B 8 took a full share, possibly more, undaunted either by the arduous nature of the work or by the unpleasant prevalence of mud. The officers rated it as one of the largest and most dependable platoons coming under their direction,[2] and the C.O. showed a disposition to look to B 8 for special service as required. From first to last a very considerable amount of work was undertaken and accomplished by the Platoon, and the casualty list, 'One, slight,' is therefore surprisingly small.

[1] Colonel Godley writes: 'The work done at Didcot was most highly (and deservedly) commended by the military authorities.'

[2] Major A. F. Walden, writing 'as one who knew them almost from the first, and who commanded at one time B Company and later the Battalion', refers to 'the extraordinarily high standard, in every sense, which B 8 maintained', and adds emphatically that it would be impossible to speak too highly of the Press Platoon.

At the Riding School, where the Army Service Corps had some considerable forage stores, guard duty was chiefly a precaution against fire. It was of course a necessary duty, but generally monotonous, the most exciting incident being provided by an A.S.C. man with a powerful inclination to slumber and a fixed idea of sleeping on the straw. Against his will he was 'persuaded' to spend the night in the Guard Room instead.

There was an occasion, about Christmas time, when the relief guard from Oxford was delayed by fog on the railway journey and arrived at Leafield [1] so late that the released guard, composed of members of B 8, missed the last train at Shipton station and spent the remainder of the night in the chilly tap-room of a neighbouring public-house.

Parties from B 8 attended all camps held during the period of its existence—Wantage, Bicester, Eynsham. In the course of a three-days camp at Wantage (1915) the residents found one morning that their statue of King Alfred had 'joined up' in the night and was wearing the brassard of the 'G.R.'s'.

The Platoon turned out to take part in the welcome accorded to Admiral Beatty when he visited Oxford, again on the following day to do similar honour to General Haig, and on another occasion to Admiral Tyrwhitt; and was present in full strength at a mass parade in the Parks one memorable Sunday (November 1916) [2] when a visit of inspection was paid by General French.

At the funeral of Mr. George Denton the Platoon paraded, under Lieut. Burnet, and lined the pathway from the cemetery entrance to the graveside. On another occasion they sent, by request, a non-commissioned officer and six privates to attend the funeral of an old soldier of the Oxford and Bucks Regiment, the military at Cowley Barracks having several funerals on that same day.

[1] 'This Leafield duty was performed by the 1st and 2nd Battalions through the winter of 1916–17, a season of exceptional severity. Much credit is due to those who volunteered for it.'—Col. A. D. Godley.

[2] 'On that day, in spite of heavy and continuous rain, 1,200 men from the two Battalions were on parade in the Parks or guarding the railway lines.'—Col. A. D. Godley.

When in 1918 there came a call for volunteers to form an East Coast Defence Corps, several members of the Press Platoon were accepted and did duty on the East Coast for three months. In view of the strictness of the conditions as to age and physical fitness for this service, proportionately B 8 did extremely well.

With the signing of the Armistice the Platoon's activities slackened, and soon ceased altogether. In due course the rifles, the ordinary service accoutrements, and the khaki uniforms (that had superseded the grey ones after the official recognition of the Corps) were handed in, and the Press Volunteer Platoon, its mission accomplished, formally and unostentatiously slipped out of existence. But not out of memory. Not a man of the Platoon will ever forget his connexion with B 8; the officers still speak of it in the highest terms; and Colonel Godley himself has written: 'I shall always be grateful to "B 8". That Platoon was distinguished throughout by its keenness and good work, and no one who had anything to do with it is likely to forget it.'

THE AMBULANCE DIVISION

The Press Division of the Oxford Corps of the St. John Ambulance Brigade was formed in January 1909, and thus had served an apprenticeship of five and a half years when, as part of the Oxford Corps, it was mobilized for War Service on 4 August 1914. The membership of the Division, beginning with 26, has never been large. The War at once drew away some to full-time service elsewhere, including Sergt. C. Foster; and by the end of September 1914 the effective strength was 13 only. This number was somewhere near the average maintained through the years of war. The late Mr. W. A. Goodger, who was honorary secretary to the Division, retained that office when he became First Divisional Officer, but relinquished the inspectorship of stores. Mr. Goodger's heart was in the work, and his habitual thoroughness, his kindliness and tact, were of inestimable value to the Division. His death, in the epidemic of 'flu' in October 1918, was felt as a personal loss by every member, and all who were able attended the funeral.

The Division's war-time activities included a full share (possibly more) of the work done by the Oxford Corps in attendances for duty as orderlies at the 3rd Southern General Hospital (the Examination Schools) and supplementary hospitals at the Town Hall, the Masonic Hall, and Durham Buildings; and in meeting convoys of wounded at the railway station, and assisting in their conveyance to the hospitals. In these latter duties a part was taken in the later years by the women's section, a Women's Nursing Division having been formed in 1917. Under Mrs. Coventon the women in various ways ministered to the wounded on arrival, and the Corps provided cigarettes and other minor comforts for those who could enjoy them. Most members possess Nursing Certificates as well as the certificate for First Aid.

With assistance from members of the Press Fire Brigade and other volunteers a very large amount of self-sacrificing work was done; more than one member is still something less robust than he should be, as a result of the arduous labours then performed at all hours of the twenty-four. The thoughtfulness of Dr. and Mrs. Coventon in supplying coffee &c. for the ambulance workers was greatly appreciated, particularly when convoys came in by night.

As the work done, though arduous, showed no great variety, not much of outstanding incident can be recorded. There was one occasion when four members of the Division, taking up an invalid for conveyance to Somerville College (then an officers' hospital), recognized in the patient a Press man, Lieut. C. D. Piper. The earliest convoys, met of course with alacrity and in the spirit of the Good Samaritan, put a strain upon benevolence by yielding chiefly wounded German prisoners! Mercy stood the test, but it was severe. Later on, when the trains brought in many wounded Belgians, the gratitude of the sufferers was in marked contrast.

On 15 January 1919, after a dinner in Queen's College Hall, several members of the Division received the Brigade's War Service badges.

Of the total number of attendances of members at the

A DEMONSTRATION

railway stations and the hospitals no statistics are available, but in one year they met 134 Red Cross trains and took 152 turns of hospital duty. The Corps as a whole, including the Press Division, from first to last moved more than 105,000 invalid soldiers.

When members were called out for these duties in the ordinary working hours of the Press, leave of absence was freely given.

THE FIRE BRIGADE

The ordinary methods of a fire brigade being of little avail against the flames of war, it might have seemed that our Press Brigade could do little more than keep the home fires within bounds. But the impulse to be up and doing was everywhere, and everywhere there was something to be done; our firemen had no reason to complain of unemployment. Some members 'joined up' very early in the War, and from first to last twenty served in His Majesty's Forces and one was engaged on National Service. To help to fill the gaps, retired brigadiers forgot their claim to leisured calm and re-enrolled; and the energy displayed by these veterans was surprising.

Some members, besides performing the usual routine duties and drills of firemen, were also drilling as members of the Volunteer Corps. Some too were also active members of the St. John Ambulance Brigade; but after Dr. Coventon's urgent appeal for more Ambulance workers practically all members of the Fire Brigade were enrolled as supernumeraries, putting in many drills with the Oxford Corps of the Ambulance Brigade at the University Gymnasium in Alfred Street. They did most valuable work too in helping to convey the wounded from Red Cross trains to the Base and other War hospitals, and in taking many turns of night duty at the hospitals, under the direction of the Ambulance Brigade.

These additional drills and duties notwithstanding, members did not cease to be firemen. In conjunction with members of the City Fire Brigade they took turns of night duty at the military hospitals; and later they did night duty regularly at City Head-quarters with the City Brigade until the end of the War. As the members of the City Brigade were drawn away for military service Captain Symonds relied more and more upon the Press Brigade standing by to supplement his decreasing forces, and the two Brigades worked together in the greatest harmony at the several serious fires which occurred in the City in the period from January to September 1917 (notably at the Y.M.C.A., George Street, and at the Riding School) and at the minor fires that occurred subsequently.

THE GARDENING ASSOCIATION

Early in 1917, when the creeping shadow of 'frightfulness' was nearing Britain's larder, those Press men who were also spare-time gardeners (which is to say, most of them), mindful that union is strength, resolved to take concerted action. Thus the University Press Gardening Association came into being; potato patches broadened out, and odds and ends of wilderness or flower bed were marked down for the production of vegetables. The land-hunger grew. In March of that year (1917) the Freemen of Oxford and the Oxford City Council granted fifteen acres of the raised portion of Port Meadow for cultivation, and of this ground a share was allotted to the Press gardeners. By the end of the month plots had been balloted for, pegging-out was in progress, and spade-work had begun. Four months later excellent results were reported, and these allotments were declared to be the best in the neighbourhood. More ground being required, early in the new year a further four and a quarter acres was conceded, and twenty-eight 10-pole plots of this new ground were allotted to the Press men. In the allocation of these plots, preference was given to men who had served in His Majesty's Forces and to such as had not already some land under cultivation.

In the second summer (1918) the menace to the nation's food supply was somewhat less alarming, but the yield from the Press men's plots showed no tendency to fall off in quality or in quantity. Then it was that there came, from 'Somewhere', the suggestion that a Food-Production Show should be promoted and the proceeds given to the popular Christmas

SOME OF THE EXHIBITS

LISTENING TO THE MUSIC

THE FIRST SHOW: 1918

Comforts Fund. The idea caught on. A group of members, meeting casually on the Port Meadow allotments, talked it over, drew up an outline of the scheme there and then, and thus launched the preparations that went merrily forward to the surprisingly successful Show of 7 September. Expectations were high: hopes of a net result of £20 were general, and modesty refrained from remonstrance with a forecast of £25. But the gardeners had struck a richer vein than they knew. Their achievements in food-production were of interest to everybody, and the thought of Christmas comforts for the exiled heroes made a powerful appeal. The Show was very heartily supported in every way, and the sum handed to the treasurer of the Comforts Fund was about £62.

After that, it was only natural that the Show should become an annual event. In 1919, the Comforts Fund being demobilized, the proceeds of the Second Show went towards the cost of the War Memorial, contributing £57. The Third Show produced the £24 still required for the Memorial, and the surplus, about £20, went to the newly formed Benevolent Fund. The Fourth Show raised about £30, which also went to the Benevolent Fund.

One of the by-products of the memorable First Show was the quarterly house-magazine, *The Clarendonian*, which, like the popular Aunt of Charley, is 'still running'.

MONEY, AND OTHER MATTERS

The need for 'silver bullets' made itself obvious in various ways. When, in July 1915, the 4½ per cent. War Loan was launched, the firm kindly put it within the power of the wage-earners to acquire £5 War Loan Certificates by means of weekly payments of 1*s.* or 2*s.* In 'Destroyer Week' (March 1918) similar facilities were given for the purchase of £5 National War Bonds and of War Savings Certificates. The response was good. The total sum invested in this way by the staff was £1,847. In the same way the firm have assisted investment in the Oxford Corporation's 6 per cent. Housing Bonds.

These, however, were investments. Money was urgently required for objects that would yield no pecuniary return.

The Christmas Comforts Fund

By Christmas 1914 the Press men serving numbered about 150, and £36 *2s. 1d.* had been collected to send a parcel to each of them. In 1915 the sum accumulated was £47 13*s.* 3*d.* and the recipients of parcels numbered about 220. In the following year, 1916, £100 1*s.* 2*d.* was raised; and in 1917 £178 9*s.* 7*d.*, the parcels numbering about 300. In 1918, although the War was over, a sum of £167 5*s.* 9*d.* was available and a goodly number of parcels or remittances was dispatched. The total amount raised for the five Christmases was £529 11*s.* 10*d.* Over £500 was spent on the 'comforts', and the balance formed the nucleus of the War Memorial Fund. Beyond these figures not much can be recorded, but the silence conceals a great deal of hard work on the part of the committee and of warm appreciation on the part of the soldiers.

Mono Parcels Fund

Besides the wholesale dispatch of parcels at Christmas by the Comforts Fund committee, other dispatches were made on smaller scale and with less regard to the almanac. The Monotype Department had its own Fund, and kept in fairly close touch with its absentees. A weekly collection of pennies in the department began in May 1915. This was supplemented by gifts and donations, and as these came in the committee 'traded with the same' and turned shillings into half-crowns. Altogether, somewhere about £70 was raised and spent; regular contributions were made to the Christmas Comforts Fund, and about 170 parcels or remittances were sent out. One parcel was returned by the Post Office; all others were duly delivered. Although the Fund existed nominally for Mono men only, generous support came from all quarters of the Press, and several of the parcels went to men from other departments.

The Institute

From the outset of the War the Institute Council was faced with problems of finance in comparison with which those of peace time were but a parlour game. Week by week the number of members away on service was growing; and a dwindling subscription list, with no corresponding reduction in expenditure, called up all the reserves of enterprise and energy. Somehow or other, new sources of revenue had to be found. A good deal of extra work fell upon all members of the Council, and especially on those of the Entertainment Committee. It was no small matter to take in hand; but great results were made possible by the ready co-operation of talent from all quarters. The Press Dramatic Society was well to the fore, and the Press Orchestra played a variety of parts. Dr. Allen gave a concert (November 1917) at which Miss Ethel McLelland sang. Other concert parties from outside who rallied round were the 'Beverleys', the 'Chestnuts', the 'Rouge et Noir', the 'Finches', and the Glee Party of the 3/4th Bn. Oxford & Bucks.

Besides covering the considerable loss on members' subscriptions and meeting the rising expenditure, these entertainments, together with Whist Drives, Card and Billiard Tournaments, Dances, &c., brought in the wherewithal to keep the Children's New Year Party from collapse, to help one or two cases of illness and adversity, and to hand over sums of money to various funds. Chief of these was our own Christmas Comforts Fund. One of the entertainments given for that Fund deserves special mention. In December 1917 Mrs. Hall and the Press Orchestra, assisted by some of the members of the Dramatic Society, performed 'Mrs. Jarley's Waxworks'. No more successful or remunerative entertainment has ever been given at the Institute. This show was repeated in the New Year to wounded soldiers in the War hospitals at the Town Hall, the Workhouse, and Somerville College. Other funds augmented by these entertainments were those of the St. John Ambulance Brigade, the Radcliffe Infirmary, the V.A.D. Hospital, the National Institute for the Blind, the Y.M.C.A., St. Dunstan's, the Blue Cross; also the Oxfordshire Prisoners of War Fund, the fund for the relief of Oxford and Bucks prisoners at Kut, our own Benevolent Fund, and the exchequers of the Press Cricket Club, Football Club, and Athletic Sports.

The Entertainment Committee assisted at the Food-Production Show in 1918, and, through the following winter, at the request of the National Service Spare Time Committee they provided a weekly Concert Party to visit each of the local hospitals.

The need for entertainments (and funds) did not cease with the War; nor did the work of the Committee or of the Dramatic Society, Orchestra, and others. The amounts raised have grown year by year. In the season 1915–16 the amount was £58 0*s.* 8*d.*; in 1916–17, £83 17*s.* 7*d.*; in 1917–18 £166 17*s.* 6*d.*; in 1918–19, £273 6*s.* 9*d.*; in 1919–20, £339 17*s.* 5*d.*—a total in five seasons of £921 19*s.* 11*d.*

The Institute itself proved a boon in many ways during the War, and not to members only. The building or parts of it were lent at times to the men of Kitchener's Army, the Fusiliers, the St. John Ambulance Brigade, and the Volunteers. In March 1917 the wounded soldiers from the local hospitals were invited to a Whist Drive, Concert, and Tea, and competed for the useful articles which were given as prizes. Men home on leave were glad to find the ''Stute' carrying on 'business as usual' in every way possible, and it seldom happened that there was no khaki to be seen anywhere on the premises.

Sport

Naturally in a time of war all outdoor games were deprived of most of their normal support. If there were any who held that our sports clubs should suspend operations altogether, the Secretary to the Delegates (Mr. C. Cannan) was not among them, and it was with his approval that efforts were made to carry on. Football practically went out, owing to the absence of players; and the football material was 'posted' to France and went into action in its own way behind the lines. Much of the cricket material also went on service abroad; but the Cricket Club and also the Bowls Club kept going, on modest programmes. 'Leave' men could generally find opportunity for a game, and the workers at home were able to take occasional relaxation in this way. It was with some of the Cricket Club's material that a match was played at Hebuterne in August 1915, between a Press Eleven and B Coy., 1/4th Oxf. & Bucks L.I. There was a risk of the bails being dislodged by missiles from the enemy's guns, but the match was played out. The Press team were L. Collier (capt.), F. P. Carter, E. Edmonds, G. W. Green, O. O. Price, S. E. Judge, A. C. Margetts, E. S. Masters, W. H. Masters, E. T. Nurser, and G. D. N. Walker.